MARRIAGE, FAMILY,
AND THE
CHRISTIAN HOME

Harold S. Martin

ISBN   978-0-9777766-9-6

Unless otherwise noted, all Scripture quotations are from the New King James Version.

Copies of this book are available from:
Brethren Revival Fellowship
P. O. Box 543
Ephrata, PA 17522

DEDICATION

This book is dedicated to my wife of nearly 60 years. She is the one who deserves credit for feeding and nurturing and often gently but firmly disciplining our six children. She read stories to them and encouraged Bible memorization. She is truly an example of the Proverbs 31 woman. "Her husband is known in the gates…[and] strength and honor are her clothing…she opens her mouth with wisdom, and on her tongue is the law of kindness. She watches over the ways of her household, and does not eat the bread of idleness. Her children rise up and call her blessed. Her husband also, and he praises her" (Proverbs 31:23-28). Her father-in-law, Harold's father (Noah Martin)—when he was nearly eighty-eight years old—said to Priscilla, *"Many daughters have done well, but you excel them all"* (Proverbs 31:29).

FOREWORD

Herbert Lockyer, in *All the Promises of the Bible*, says, "No matter how one may look at the Bible…its authorship is divine, its historicity is unquestioned, and its teachings are eminently spiritual. Yet although its tone is so high and lofty, it is the most practical book in the world when it comes to dealing with the common and ordinary relationships of life. It is indispensable in that it touches life at every point. This is especially true when it deals with love and romance, courtship and marriage, [and] home and parenthood. No phase of marital life is omitted" (page 366).

America is suffering because many of its *homes* are being destroyed. The Bible declares that the spiritual health of families is one of the keys to the health of a nation and of society. The Bible lifts up the sanctity of marriage to a level that was unknown in ancient times, and many of America's founding fathers accepted that standard. Today those who embrace secularism and hedonism are destroying the family.

Over the years I have preached sermons on good family relationships, and also have given several series of lectures on the home and family. Bringing up a family is a large task. I don't have all the answers, and most of us have made some mistakes, but by the grace of God, and by honest attempts to live by the principles of God's Word, *we can have* healthy family relationships.

My wife, Priscilla, is an efficient helpmeet, a constant companion, and the joy of my heart. All our children, as far as we know, embrace our general values. We have six children, twenty-seven grandchildren, and one great grand child. Our youngest daughter, Berdene, at the age of 32, has been called home to the eternal world. Also, three of our grandchildren have departed this life.

God has a plan for family happiness and success. His plan is explained in Psalm 103:17-18—*"But the mercy of the LORD is from everlasting to everlasting on those who fear Him, and His righteousness to children's children, to such as keep His covenant, and to those who remember His commandments to do them."* This is God's promise to parents, to their children, and to their grandchildren.

The vital principles set forth in this study are based on Bible teachings, and they work because they are *God's* principles. Those who seek to live by the biblical standards will find that indeed they do work.

This book is written for those who are already married, as well as for those who are contemplating marriage. The goal is to give married couples a new understanding of problems that arise in the home, and to help those who are planning to marry—to make wise decisions about whom to marry and how to stay married.

The lessons in this book on *Marriage, Family, and the Christian Home* are the result of combining great principles of Bible truth with common sense and practical experience. It is my hope that reading this book will be a refreshing and an encouraging experience for young families just starting out, and for those families that are seasoned and mature.

Harold S. Martin
26 United Zion Circle
Lititz, PA 17543

November 1, 2008

TABLE OF CONTENTS
Marriage, Family, and the Christian Home

INTRODUCTION

MARRIAGE, FAMILY, AND THE
CHRISTIAN HOME

There is a war being waged against the family today. Value-systems in society are dramatically changing. Television is the leading moral influence in the typical American home, and more and more people in our churches are choosing to place themselves under its influence. Values are changing regarding household leadership styles, child raising practices, sexual attitudes, and marital arrangements.

Some of the forces which lie behind the war on the family include the *immoral impact of television*, the *advent of no-fault divorce laws*, the *radical feminist movement*, the *homosexual revolution*, and the *acceptance of genetic engineering*. These forces have all affected the break-down in discipline, the forsaking of the family altar, and the tendency to discard motherhood as a blessed career.

No matter where one turns to find statistics, the picture of marriage nationwide is not pretty. Roughly half of all marriages in the United States end in divorce. Cohabitation has increased by more than 500% in the last 20 years. Children in the twenty-first century have at least a 50-50 chance of growing up in single-parent households.

The philosophy which is advocated by multitudes today is that fathers are bad, moms need to work outside the home, and *if they are home* they are unhappy. Marriage is boring; teenagers are smarter than their parents, clergy are bumbling hypocrites, sex outside of marriage is not wrong unless it is forced, and profanity is acceptable. Surely these attitudes indicate a major change from the beliefs held by earlier generations in American society.

One issue that needs to be settled is the question, "What is *a family*?" One association defines a family as "two or more people who reside under the same roof and have a commitment to the future." A careful biblical definition, by way of contrast, emphatically implies that *a family* is "a unit comprised of persons who are related by blood, by marriage, or by adoption—with a male father and a female mother who have made a binding covenant for life."

The biblical definition rules out *apartment marriages* (a fellow and a girl temporarily live together until one partner tires of the other, or until they decide to marry). It eliminates *bigamous liaisons* (an arrangement whereby two women are living with one man). It rules out *communal living* (a kind of group set-up in which there are no husband-wife covenants but each is free to cohabit with the other). It excludes *homosexual partnerships* (lesbians or male homosexuals who live together and perhaps even make a covenant, and may also adopt children.)

What influences are affecting the family? Only a small percentage of our nation's households consist of *"the ideal family"*—a working father, a stay-at-home mother, and one or more legitimate children. Many of our nation's households are merely persons of the opposite sex sharing living quarters, having decided to simply live together without making the commitment of marriage. *The influences that have led to these conditions are at least four in number:*

1) *Industrialization*—the move from the farm to cities and towns. Families now tend to be more fragmented, with the various members of the family going their own ways.

2) *Secularism*—the system of belief which rejects the need for true religious devotion. God is left out of the individual life and one's daily activities.

3) *Humanism*—the belief that mankind evolved over millions of years, and that humans can solve their problems if given enough time and education. Moral right and wrong is based on what the majority thinks.

4) *Materialism*—the view which implies that material things can satisfy the deepest needs of the human heart. The materialist believes that being wealthy and having a nice house will bring happiness.

Nearly all of Western civilization has drifted far from the standards for home and family that are given in the Bible. Yet in spite of the adultery and premarital sex and single-parent houscholds and child abuse—many people still hope to establish stable home environments which will lead to the survival of the family.

Parents *can have* happy families if they really want them. God's principles for a strong and happy home are easy to understand, but they are often difficult to obey. We must diligently teach biblical values to those who are younger. God's standards include the following:

1) The home must be committed to Jesus Christ, rather than to self-fulfillment and personal rights.

2) Persons who marry must see marriage as an ongoing lifetime commitment.

3) It is necessary to make honest apologies to one's spouse when there are failures.

4) Married couples need to choose a modest living standard in order to make ends meet financially.

This book is not intended to be a collection of fancy formulas which will immediately bring good results. Our goal is to clarify God's principles, which if followed, will bring into being strong families and happy households.

We will look at the *Biblical Basis for Marriage and Family*, some principles related to *Courtship, Engagement, and the Wedding*, the *Roles of Husband, Wife, and Children*, the *Necessity for Adjustment in Marriage*, and a focus on *Practical Pointers for Child Training*.

It is important to note that in our day almost *every child in the world* knows the name "Harry Potter," while at the same time, the name of Jesus is foreign to multitudes. And out of the more than six billion people living on earth, one-third of the population is less than fifteen years old.

Most young persons look forward to finding a marriage partner and someday becoming parents and raising a family of children. Outside of the decision to choose Jesus Christ as Lord of one's life—the right choice of a marriage partner is the most important decision one will ever make. It seems that many today plan more carefully the details of the wedding event itself, than they do for the marriage.

Howard and Jeanne Hendricks observe that many marriages today are "like flies on a windowpane: *those out* want in and *those in* want out." In addition, they say that "marriage has never been more popular, and never more perverted; marriages may be made in heaven, but the maintenance work is done on earth."[1]

Marriage is much more than a contract. Marriage is a *covenant*—and it is the most intimate human relationship into which two human beings can enter. A marriage can be beautiful, but the beauty can be lasting only when it is a three-some arrangement—the husband, wife, and the Lord Jesus. It is important that all biblical commands related to marriage are accepted as the standard by which to live.

---

[1] *Husbands and Wives*, Howard and Jeanne Hendricks, page 97.

Chapter 1

THE BIBLICAL BASIS FOR MARRIAGE
AND THE FAMILY

Most people would like to have an obedient and vibrant and happy family. They would like to have a devoted spouse and model children who are exemplary in behavior, and who bring joy to the home. The price required is obedience to God's recipe as given in the Bible.

1. The Divine Origin of the Family

Marriage is a union between a man and a woman, sanctified by God as a means of maintaining family life. The idea of marriage was ordained by God in His instruction to Adam, that a man should leave his father and mother, and that he and his wife should be as one flesh. The key Bible passage is Genesis 2:24, "Therefore a man shall leave his father and mother and be joined to his wife, and they shall become one flesh." Note some conclusions gleaned from Genesis 2:24—

a) Marriage is to be *monogamous* (one man/one woman, a man and "his wife," not "his wives."

b) Marriage is to be *permanent* ("joined to" speaks of a binding commitment, like epoxy glue).

c) Marriage is to be *heterosexual* (given in the context of a man and a woman—Adam and Eve, not Adam and Steve).

d) Marriage is to be *a separate unit* ("leave" means "to abandon the former relationship").

The highest, purest, and happiest form of human relationship has always been that which God instituted—the uniting of one man and one woman in a binding marriage commitment for life. If the human family had observed this standard down through the years, the *scourge of AIDS* would be unknown! God intends some to remain single. Singleness allows for more dedicated service in the Lord's work (1 Corinthians 7:32-34), but remaining single is the exception rather than the rule. Marriage is a good thing, yet marriage is not everything.

Marriage is so sacred, that in Ephesians 5:25-32, it is compared to the relationship between the believer and Christ. Three of the Ten Commandments have a direct reference to the home and family—the 5th Commandment (honor your father and your mother); the 7th Commandment (you shall not commit adultery); and the 10th Commandment (you shall not covet...your neighbor's wife).

2. The American Custom of Dating

Dating, as a medium by which boy meets girl, is an American social invention. Dating is a period of finding. Some try to distinguish between "courtship" and "dating," but that tends to be a matter of semantics—a play on words.

In some countries, the bridal couple does not see each other until the day of the wedding. Among certain tribes, the prospective husband must work for several years in order to pay a dowry for his bride, just like Jacob did many years ago in Mesopotamia. In the United States, most young people spend some time in each other's presence, agreeing to meet each other at a certain time, and planning activities that will be experienced together.

The Bible encourages young men and women to share life together as married partners. And since it is unwise for people suddenly to marry—without ever having paid any attention to each other and without being mutually attracted and happy together, we encourage a period of courtship among those who are planning to marry.

The courtship period affords two persons the opportunity to study at close range the attitudes and conduct and true worth of their special friends. It is proper to test the personalities of potential mates—and therefore, even though dating is primarily a social custom—it can produce good results if it is conducted discreetly.

There are many dangers and pitfalls for dating couples during the years of courtship. The most portending danger is related to habits that can lead to sexual intimacy. The primary reason why many marriages end in disaster, is because during courtship, the couple becomes too engrossed in their *physical attraction* for each other—and they don't get to know each other *as persons*—because the sex attraction becomes predominant.

Young men should take the lead in maintaining sexual purity, but if they fail to do that, the young lady should not tolerate attempts by the male friend to push for more intimate forms of bodily contact. To the female partner in a courting relationship, please accept this advice: If the young man is demanding more intimacies he is obviously not very mature. Young women should, in that case, tell "junior" to pack his diapers and go back to his mother until he learns how to treat a woman with respect and dignity.

Two people just cannot really get to know each other as persons—if sex is the primary focus of the relationship. It is very easy to overlook even obvious personality defects if passions are aroused, because so much pleasurable emotion comes from the activities of being involved in close bodily contact. After all, in the moments of heated passion, who cares about personality defects?

The sex experience is beautiful and meaningful and right—but only when it functions in the role that God has designed for it—and that is within the bounds of true and honorable and committed marriage (Hebrews 13:4).

3. God's Purposes for Marriage

The Scriptures give reasons why God has established the marriage relationship. For family life to function as God our Creator intended, His purposes should be kept in mind.

a) *The propagation of the race.* Genesis 1:28 says that humans are to be fruitful and multiply and fill the earth. The Hebrew grammatical structure of the sentence indicates that the words "be fruitful" and "multiply" and "fill"—are not commands, but are promises of God's blessing upon families.

b) *The elimination of solitude and loneliness.* Marriage provides an intimate companionship between two people. Genesis 2:18 says that "It is not good that man should be alone; I will make him a helper comparable to him."

c) *The provision of a deterrent to immorality.* The New Testament clearly states that one of the purposes for marriage is to provide a wholesome release for the sex drive. First Corinthians 7:2 says, "Nevertheless, to avoid fornication, let every man have his own wife, and let every woman have her own husband" (KJV).

d) *The illustration of a spiritual marriage.* We are told in Ephesians 5:23 that "the husband is head of the wife, as also Christ is head of the church." Also, husbands are to love their wives, and wives are to be subject to their husbands. This relationship is an illustration of the way we are parts of the body of Christ (Ephesians 5:32).

e) *The instruction of children in the ways of God.* We learn in Ephesians 6:4 that parents are not to provoke their children to wrath, but are to "bring them up in the training and admonition of the Lord."

Some of these factors will be discussed in more detail as we progress in our studies throughout the book.

4. The Permanence of Marriage

The New Testament teaches that marriage is intended for a lifetime. Marriage is always to be permanent. Initiating a divorce is always prohibited.

One who sues for a divorce *violates* the command to live peaceably with others "as much as depends on you" (Romans 12:18); *fails to observe* the command to forgive "seventy times seven times" (Matthew 18:22); *disregards* the "vow" (Ecclesiastes 5:5) for better or for worse; and *ignores* the clear prohibition against going to courts of law to get justice from fellow Christians (1 Corinthians 6:7).

There are seven New Testament passages that deal with the permanency of marriage. They are:

Matthew 5:31-32
Matthew 19:3-8
Mark 10:1-12
Luke 16:18
Romans 7:2-3
1 Corinthians 7:10
1 Corinthians 7:39

All of the above portions of Scripture when taken together *give overwhelming and undisputed evidence for the permanency of marriage*. The only possible loophole for "putting away" (divorcing) a married partner, is the exception clause in Matthew 19:9 and Matthew 5:32, where the KJV rendering of Matthew 19:9 reads, "Whoever shall put away his wife, *except it be fornication*, and shall marry another, commits adultery." Most of the more recent translations say, "Whoever divorces his wife, *except for sexual immorality*,

19

and marries another, commits adultery" (NKJV). The NRSV says, *"except for unchastity,"* and the NIV says, *"except for marital unfaithfulness."*

There are *three* basic interpretations of the New Testament exception clause:

The *Patristic* View—(held by the faithful early church leaders) says that if one suffered the misfortune of divorce, remarriage was not permitted regardless of the cause of the breakup. The exception grammatically can only apply to the divorcing. There is no exception for remarriage. Sexual unfaithfulness may be a sufficient cause for divorce but is not a legitimate reason for remarriage. (This is a valid interpretation of the passage.)

The *Betrothal View*—(held by many believers over the years) says that the exception refers *not to* a marriage divorce *but to* an engagement divorce. Betrothal (or "engagement") among Orientals was a bond almost as binding as marriage itself, and therefore it took a bill of divorcement to break the marriage. A young woman who is merely engaged is never called a "wife" in our Western society, but in the mid-East, even before the marriage is consummated, the woman is called a "wife."

The exception clause, *according to this view*, refers to the breaking of an engagement when sexual immorality (fornication) has occurred. When Jesus said, "except it be for fornication," He was saying that if the young man discovered that his espoused wife (the girl he was going to marry) had been immoral before the marriage (that is, if she committed fornication during the engagement period), he could return the girl to her father along with a legal divorce document. (Matthew's Jewish Christian readers would very well have understood this exception.)

The *Erasmian View*—(the typical 20th century Protestant and evangelical view) says that Jesus allows divorce *and* remarriage in the case of adultery, and desertion, and that other trivial reasons were also sufficient causes for divorce and remarriage. Erasmus (died 1536) was a humanist who reasoned that it would be unfair to expect one who is divorced not to have the freedom to remarry. (This is the only view that allows for remarriage of the divorced person; it is based totally on human reasoning.)

It is true that many divorce cases are really tangled, and that each situation is a little different from the other, but Jesus clearly says that God never intended that marriages should ever be broken. Marriage is a permanent relationship. Divorce does not dissolve the marriage union as death does, for if it did, it would be unnecessary for Jesus to say, "and whoever marries a woman who is divorced commits adultery" (Matthew 5:32b). For this reason, I have chosen over the years not to perform a marriage ceremony for anyone who has a former living companion.

The faithful church throughout its history held that marriage "is an indissoluble bond," and that "divorce, with the implicit right of remarriage, was not an option for Christian couples" (See *Christianity Today*, December 14, 1992.). In addition, *the Anabaptists have historically "recognized adultery as legitimate grounds for divorce on the basis of Matthew 5:32, but generally forbade remarriage following divorce"* (documented in the December 14, 1992 *Christianity Today* article).

We can never say to divorced and remarried people, that there is no way. There is a way! The church has always received divorced and remarried people—if they separated and lived chaste lives apart from each other.

Jesus said that to follow Him might involve breaks in family relations. To take such a step *is hard*, but the way of the transgressor has always been hard.

There is *no easy solution* when divorced people remarry while their original partner is still living—and then they choose to take the biblical way.

Some say, "But is it right to break up a family relationship (in the case of divorced and remarried people) and place the children out of the normal situation with father and mother?" It is best to think of it this way: *If one home is deliberately broken up for the cause of biblical obedience— and the remarried man and woman decide to live separately, that is nothing compared to the thousands of homes which are broken up each year by divorce because of strife, bickering, sexual unfaithfulness, and other schemes of Satan.* In such situations tens of thousands of children must adjust to living alone with the mother, or in some kind of broken arrangement and setting.

Marriage is a serious step. The vows are recorded in heaven. Marriage is a lifetime contract. "What therefore God has joined together, let not man put asunder."

Every young couple going to the marriage altar *must resolve to make the marriage work*. One of the reasons for the skyrocketing divorce rate—*is the loss of determination to stay married.*

Marriage is a sacred, inviolable, divine institution which shall not be broken except by death. It is not merely a common civil contract. It is a mystical union between a man and a woman so close, so intimate, and so spiritually significant, that Jesus declares "the two become one flesh."

Chapter 2

COURTSHIP, ENGAGEMENT, THE WEDDING

Most young people look forward to marriage and to having a happy family, but not as many seem willing to pay the price required for that kind of home.

There are many young persons who really would like to have *a model family*. Their goal is to have a devoted wife, an outstanding husband, and model children who are exemplary in behavior and a joy to live with.

The price required for such a family is obedience to God's recipe for yielding an outstanding family. The recipe begins with the process of courtship and dating.

Marriage is not a human custom that gradually came to be accepted during early human history. Marriage is a sacred institution intended to be a lifetime proposition. Jesus says that God *"made them male and female, and said, For this cause shall a man leave father and mother, and shall cleave to his wife, and they twain shall be one flesh"* (Matthew 19:4-5, quoting Genesis 2:24).

1. Wholesome Courtship

The Bible encourages people to marry—and certainly it is inadvisable for men and women to suddenly marry, without getting to know each other. It is a fact that the emotional poise and maturity of your married partner will have much to do with the character of your home.

Many marriages are wrecked because two young people rush into the marriage relationship on the basis of a strong infatuation with the partner's outward charms.

So God approves courtship and dating—but there are some instructions that need to be passed along to youth.

a. The dangers of courtship

There are many snares that can mislead during the years of courtship, but the most menacing danger is related to *habits which can lead to sexual intimacy*.

The primary reason why many marriages fail and lead to divorce—is because the couple during courtship days has become so involved in *their physical attraction* for each other that they did not really get to know each other's real personality traits. The pleasurable feelings associated with touching and squeezing, are so powerful that it is very easy to overlook even obvious defects of character. At those moments, when the passions are aroused, traits of character are generally not on the minds of the man and woman.

The sex experience is approved only within the bonds of a true and honorable marriage. *Why within marriage?* Because God knows that the physical relationship between a man and a woman, even in times of modern birth control methods, may lead to the birth of a child—and He knows that the child will most likely get proper nurture only within the setting of a venerable marriage.

It is in light of this principle that God says, *"Marriage is honorable among all, and the bed undefiled, but fornicators and adulterers God will judge"* (Hebrews 13:4).

In the Bible, *fornication* (sex experience before one is married) is classified as being equal to stealing and murder and idolatry. Most Christians would never think of committing murder—taking the life of another person—but God says that fornication is equally wicked.

What most people during courtship don't seem to understand—is that touching and embracing (necking and petting) *are simple acts* designed to pave the way to excite the passions for the ultimate act of *fornication*. Step by step—if these habits are started, you'll likely push back the barriers of what you permit—until it is almost impossible to avoid the act of sexual intercourse.

Many young persons don't seem to recognize the principle in human behavior which is known as "the moral law of diminishing returns." The law simply says (when related to courtship practices) *that once* a couple has proceeded to one level of intimacy, it is almost impossible to return to a less intimate level. The couple who progresses from holding hands to the act of touching and embracing—can scarcely ever return to the less intimate level in the relationship and be satisfied.

And so a dating couple should enjoy each other's presence—carefully avoiding familiar intimacies that could tempt each other beyond the power of self-control. The people who can't seem to get enough of each other before marriage (exhibiting behavior that shows signs of being overly intimate with each other)—are often the very ones who have all kinds of conflicts after marriage.

One of the best safeguards to a pure courtship is a well-planned date—an evening filled with activities that are all planned—things to do and places to go that are planned in advance.

1) Visit the homes of lonely people in your community, especially the aged and widows and shut-ins. They enjoy having a group of energetic young people singing a song, engaging in conversation, reading a portion from the Bible, or letting a word of testimony.

2) Plan activities with the family in the home of either of the courting couple. Spend time together cooking a meal, making candy, popping corn, looking at pictures, singing from the hymnbook, or playing simple games.

3) Spend at least part of each dating period, reading and discussing a passage of Scripture. Both can agree to read the same portion of the Bible at the same time each evening of the week. There's something fascinating about knowing that your special friend is doing the same thing you are doing at exactly the same time, even though separated by many miles.

These are things to do, and places to go, in order to make your courtship constructive and filled with purpose.

b. The choice of courtship

The Scriptures are clear: Believers are not to even consider marriage with unbelievers under any circumstances at all. The Law in Israel forbade intermarriage with persons from the non-Jewish nations round about them (Deuteronomy 7:3). We are not to marry pagans. Believers are not to give their *daughters* to unbelieving boys or their *sons* to unbelieving girls. The New Testament commands the same thing. We are not to "be unequally yoked together with unbelievers" (2 Corinthians 6:14).

And so to those who are not yet married—we must say this: Those who seek your hand in marriage might be generous and well-trained and handsome—but unless they are children of God by faith in Jesus Christ (not necessarily members of your church), and are concerned about obedience to the Scriptures (and give clear evidence of knowing the Lord)—you must not even consider dating [courting] them. Failure to observe this basic law of God has led to shipwreck in thousands of homes—and any girl who marries a young man with the idea that she will change his undesirable traits after the ceremony, is only inviting disaster!

If a person is not honest and trustworthy before the

wedding day, the words of a marriage ceremony will not change him. If he is careless about handling money before marriage, he will likely exhibit the same characteristics in later months and years.

There are other instructions related to choosing a good partner. The question arises, "How can I know when I'm in love with the right person?" There is no formula that can accurately answer the question—but there are some statements that will be true if you are intended for each other:

1) There will be a feeling that you've been lifted to a higher spiritual level through the association with your special friend. One young man said, "Every time I'm with her, she inspires me to become a better person."

2) You will have confidence and trust in your special friend, and will not really have a desire to date other persons. True love creates a "we" feeling.

3) You will want to see and meet and know your partner's parents, brothers, sisters, and relatives and friends.

4) You will have respect for the one you love—respect for that person's beliefs and convictions and moral standards. These things will be more important than his or her physical attractiveness.

5) You will be lonely when circumstances require the two of you to be separated. You will long for the day and the hour when you can be together again.

6) You will hurt when your special friend is hurt or criticized. You will rush to the defense of your friend and seek to support him (or her).

7) You will want your children to have the character qualities and attitudes which are evident in the life of your special friend.

If each of you is bubbling over with these seven characteristics, it is quite evident that love between the two of you is really growing. And remember that true love can thrive without physical contact. If you can't be together without hugging and holding and squeezing—something is wrong. The basis for your companionship is too shallow. Your interest must be in *the total person*, not merely in his or her *physical charms*.

If you took a trip together shortly after your marriage—and you were in a car accident—and *the body* of the girl (the boy) you just married, is really battered—and her face is re-arranged—and the doctor says "She will never quite be the same"—would you still be able to love her, and to take care of her? True love is concerned about the total well-being of the potential partner, and is not merely a romantic dream about spending eternity in each other's arms!

2. Virtuous Engagement

All of us have read the account of the engagement of Joseph and Mary, as it is given in Matthew 1:18-25. "Engagement" is a definite mutual agreement between a courting couple, stating that they will *plan for* and *look forward to* marriage. They prepare for marriage by further testing their love, further learning to make adjustments, seeking to correct faults, and making plans for the wedding day.

The couple should only enter into the betrothal period after much prayer, and with the full confidence that God has been leading. There's a new joy and thrill that comes when planning things together—thinking about the future together. This new, closer companionship will help determine whether your partner's love is really genuine, or whether it is only a clever imitation.

Sometimes when a young man becomes engaged, he thinks that because the matter of whom he is going to marry has been settled—now he can relax and let his ordinary behavior surface. He may have previously been play-acting. For this reason, sometimes, one (or both) of the partners realizes that the engagement was a mistake (and this is not to encourage breaking engagements)—yet while engagements should not be taken lightly, it is far better to break an engagement than to seek a divorce after marriage.

a. Qualities that should surface during engagement
--a prospective marriage partner should have a strong faith in God and should accept the teachings of the Bible as his rule for life—including the practices of nonconformity and nonresistance.

--he should possess self-confidence, not with an air of superiority, thinking he knows it all, but with a positive feeling that he his going to meet the issues of life, and each day seek to work through problems that may arise.

--he should manifest self-discipline, exercising reasonable control over his temper, his words, and his bodily appetites.

--he should have ambition and purpose, showing a sense of responsibility toward work, toward performing his duties, and toward getting things done on time.

--he should be willing to admit his mistakes, and take responsibility for them—and vow to profit from them.

--he should have mature ideas about how to handle money; he should not be a miser who saves every penny, nor should he be a careless spender—spending everything as fast as he earns it.

--he should reflect a deep sense of respect for his home, his parents, his grandparents, and his brothers and sisters.

And of course, any person who looks for those qualities in a potential marriage companion, should work diligently to develop those same qualities in his/her own life.

b. Purposes for the engagement period

Engagement is a time when you prove your love, and guarantee that you are a team, and are both going in the same direction

--It is a time when you discover in each other an increasing companionship and a growing respect and admiration for each other.

--It is a time when you make plans for the wedding and the household that will be established.

--It is a time when you discuss such matters as how the money will be handled, how family worship will be conducted, where you will live, and how much time you will spend in each of the parent's homes. It is wise not to live at either parental home. The command to "leave" father and mother means to abandon the former relationship; it does not mean that we dishonor father and mother.

--It is a time for both of you to think about all the responsibilities that are involved in marriage. Marriage means earning a living. It means taking care of children when they come. For the husband it means being the head of the household and bringing home a paycheck to pay the bills that will pile up with regularity. For the wife it means being a guide within the home, and being a good homemaker. It means assuming one's normal duties toward the church, the nation, the state, and the community.

--It is a time when you should learn about the more intimate things of marriage, including sexual activity and the birth of children. Counsel with someone in whom you have confidence and speak about the details. A helpful book on the subject [from a Christian perspective, for persons who will soon marry] is *"Sexual Understanding in Marriage"* by Herbert J. Miles.

There is no need to try and establish a definite age for courtship, engagement, and marriage. Some people mature much earlier than others, and some never seem to mature. Nevertheless, it should be emphasized that marriage is not for those who are immature.

It is very important also to remember that just because you are engaged, does not mean that you are free to explore each other's bodies. Sexual relationships are for cementing the marriage relationship into a strong and permanent bond.

Pre-marital sex not only violates God's prohibition against engaging in *fornication* (1 Corinthians 6:13,18; Galatians 5:19; Ephesians 5:3; Colossians 3:5; 1 Thessalonians 4:3), but those who have been free with sexual relationships before marriage, are more likely to later sense guilt, and find it easier to follow a pattern of promiscuity after marriage.

3. Christ-honoring Weddings

When it comes time to plan the wedding, determine to let the occasion be marked by reverence, simplicity, and modesty. The money spent for a showy wedding is not an investment that will pay dividends; it is money spent that is gone forever. The wedding is to be a worshipful experience which should be an example to the unsaved world.

The wedding is an important ceremony because marriage is a sacred event. Jesus says that at the time of marriage, the couple leaves father and mother and they cleave to each other. They are no more two, but one flesh (Matthew 19:6). Just as Satan tries to take *Christ* out of Christmas and the *resurrection* out of Easter, so he seeks to take *the deeper spiritual essence* out of the wedding ceremony and put trivia there instead.

a. The wedding event is often lavish and expensive

You are engaged to be married, and so there will soon be plans for the wedding day. Should you have a simple ceremony, or an elaborate one? Will you invite lots of guests, or just a few of your close friends? Will you write your own vows, or have the minister use standard vows?

The formal wedding today, in many circles, involves decorations, gowns, formal suits, invitations, postage, pictures, and a reception—so that the cost often falls between $3,000 and $10,000, and even more. Yet we are aware that a wedding ceremony can be beautiful and sacred without blindly following the routine cultural patterns.

There are ways to keep the cost of a wedding in a more moderate range. Here are some suggestions.

1) Write your own personal notes of invitation instead of sending expensive engraved invitations.

2) Consider limiting the reception to a light snack instead of a full meal. Weddings would be a lot more *Christian* if they were a lot less *elaborate*!

3) Buy (or make) a nice street-length dress for the bride, and wear it occasionally after the wedding day.

4) Have only a limited number of attendants for the wedding ceremony, and request that the attendants wear clothing which they can wear after the wedding day.

There is beauty in simplicity. A wedding should not be a fashion show. It is to be one of the most sacred of all Christian services. The serious purpose of binding two hearts and lives together for a lifetime of home-building, must not be lost in the midst of the formality and display of a grandiose wedding procedure. It does not cost much to walk to the front of a church auditorium, and seriously repeat the marriage vows, and then kneel together and pray.

b. The wedding event is often built around the bride

The typical wedding in many cultures is saturated with matriarchcalism. It centers on the bride, and thus violates the Bible principle of *mutual* love and dignity that should surround both parties in a marriage.

There are many resources today that are designed to help couples plan for their wedding day. If you check the area marked "wedding supplies and services"—in the yellow pages of your phone book—there will be a long list of businesses described as bakers, balloonists, engravers, florists, musicians, photographers, video recorders, sellers of bridal gowns, renters of formal attire, and a host of other services.

In some [even conservative] church circles, the wedding format is often similar to what is described in the following paragraphs:

The people begin to arrive in the church building; there is quiet pre-ceremonial music; the ushers seat the women; the men tag along behind like frightened little puppy dogs. After a few musical selections, the clergy, the groom, and the best man appear from somewhere at the front of the church auditorium. Then, down the center aisle come some sweet little girls carrying flowers; then follow some older girls clad in beautiful dresses (often immodestly designed); and finally—the big, most important and momentous occasion arrives! In comes the bride and everyone stands to see and to admire her!

All eyes watch the bride's movements very carefully. After someone "gives" the bride away, the groom takes his place by her side. The people sit down—and from that point the ceremony is in charge of the officiating minister.

It would be much more in keeping with *mutual* love if the bride and the groom would walk into the auditorium together—or even for the bride to come via one door with her parents, and the groom come via another door with his parents—and the two meet together at the altar, facing the minister in charge.

After the ceremony the newly married couple should be allowed to greet guests, to enjoy the reception meal together with friends and relatives, without the asininity of tapping glasses—and then leave the scene of the wedding in peace, with the joyful echo of the marriage vows ringing in their ears, and the good wishes of their friends lingering in their hearts.

When two people stand side by side and promise to love and cherish each other until death separates them— it's not hard to believe that the angels in heaven hush their songs for a while, and stand in awe as they listen to the solemn vows.

May God help each young person to find joy in living, whether your lot in life involves marriage, or whether in the providence of God you happen to remain single.

To those who have never married, and you are somewhat older, the right person *might still appear* on the scene, but if not, don't become discouraged. As one of our unmarried pastor friends says, "It's better *to want* what you don't have than *to have* what you don't want!"

Chapter 3

GUIDELINES FOR A SUCCESSFUL MARRIAGE
(A message given at the marriage ceremony)

This is a happy occasion, a time when these two young people have presented themselves to be joined together in holy marriage. Their desire is to establish a *Christian* home. I say "Christian" home because John and Jill have chosen to take seriously their commitment to Christ and the church.

The message of the gospel of Christ is that all of us have sinned; none can obtain a right standing with God by his own efforts. Our motives, desires, and drives—by nature, are biased toward wrong. The Good News is that Jesus died as a Substitute for us, and that God credits His death to our account—when we believe on Him, repent of our sins, and make a covenant in Christian baptism to live for Him. And in making this commitment, we become part of a family—the church of the living God—comprised of people in many lands, who seek to live by the Scriptures. We find nurture and friendship and support in our local congregations, which help us to continue on faithfully in the Christian life.

Those who come to Jesus by simple faith—*can break free* from the bonds of sin, and *can experience* life in all its fullness, and *will more and more* become persons with new goals and new ambitions in life. Your goal and ambition at this point in your lives is to establish a Christian home. And since marriage is a relationship ordained by God, it is altogether fitting that we look to God's Word for instructions concerning the marriage relationship.

Ephesians 5:21-33 says, *"Submitting to one another in the fear of God. Wives, submit to your own husbands, as to the Lord. For the husband is head of the wife, as also Christ is head of the church; and He is the Savior of the body. Therefore, just as the church is subject to Christ, so let the wives be to their own husbands in everything. Husbands, love your wives, just as Christ also loved the church and gave Himself for her, that He might sanctify and cleanse her with the washing of water by the word, that He might present her to Himself a glorious church, not having spot or wrinkle or any such thing, but that she should be holy and without blemish. So husbands ought to love their own wives as their own bodies; he who loves his wife loves himself. For no one ever hated his own flesh, but nourishes and cherishes it, just as the Lord does the church. We are members of His body, of His flesh, and of His bones. 'For this reason a man shall leave his father and mother and be joined to his wife, and the two shall become one flesh.' This is a great mystery, but I speak concerning Christ and the church. Nevertheless let each one of you in particular so love his own wife as himself, and let the wife see that she respects her husband."*

These words from the New Testament contain some of the most helpful guidelines one could find anywhere for a successful marriage.

1. Accept Your Proper Role in the Home

The Bible teaches that in the Christian family unit—the head of the home is the Lord Jesus Christ. He is the head of the house; the unseen Guest at every meal; the silent Listener to every conversation. Under His headship each has a duty (a role), and the husband's duty is to lead and direct in the home—justly, fairly, and kindly.

To the husband, God speaks about *leadership*. It is the husband's responsibility to see that thanks is offered at each meal-time. It is the husband's responsibility to take the lead in disciplining children. It is the husband's responsibility to be the financial provider for the family. He is not to use his authority to get his way, to dominate, or to bully. Men who let these responsibilities fall on the slender shoulders of their wives—are sissies and quitters—and ought to learn what it means to be a man of spiritual strength.

To the wife, God speaks about *homemaking*. Titus 2:4-5 says that the older women should "admonish the young women to love their husbands, to love their children, to be discreet, chaste, homemakers, good, obedient to their own husbands." Therefore it is the wife's responsibility to see that the meals are tasty and well prepared. It is one of her responsibilities to frequently encourage her husband with words of appreciation. It is the wife's responsibility to teach and love and comfort and nurture the children, if God chooses to send children into the marriage union.

Accepting one's proper role implies that the wife should graciously submit to her husband's leadership, and that the husband should exercise that leadership with consideration and patience. Every home, like any other team, if it is going to be operated successfully—must have a captain, and God says that the captain of the family team is to be the husband. This does not mean that the husband is to become severe and demanding—and insisting that his wife must come running whenever he issues an order.

The husband who loves his wife as his own body *tempers his leadership responsibility* with tenderness and love. In marriage, some tough final decisions will need to be made—and they should be discussed together—but the husband must make the final decision and he must be accountable for it. So the submissive wife is free—liberated from the emotional burden of final decision making.

2. Practice the Love Commandment

Jesus said, "This is My commandment, that you love one another as I have loved you" (John 15:12). The word for "love" is "agape." This is not a gushy, syrupy kind of love that makes a big fuss over other people—and tries to act nice and puts on a bluff. Agape love is a disciplined love—the quality that helps others by doing things on time, by being loyal and dependable, and by being quick to forgive when differences arise. Agape love is not easily provoked. It does not flare up at the slightest provocation—when the car won't start or the fish won't bite or the meals are not ready on time. Agape love exercises forbearance.

The possibilities for happiness within marriage are very great, but it is important that both of you realize that marriage is not the cure for all ills. You will soon learn that the words "marriage" and "heaven" are not terms describing the same thing. Marriage is not a cure for all ills. There are many adjustments to make. Young people sometimes seem to think that finding the right person, and entering into the marriage relationship with that person, will be the answer to all life's problems—and that both will live happily ever after! The fact is, married partners must persevere at growing together as persons, and constantly keep on working at building good relationships. To use an illustration: Many young persons view marriage as a gift-wrapped box filled with lots of goodies which will bring them happiness. But marriage is really like an empty box into which you put things—such as sacrifice, and love, and commitment, and going the second mile—and *these things* will bring success.

It is only after marriage that many of the graces of character in your partner's life begin to appear. You will discover some beautiful gems in the character of the other that you never saw before. By the same token, it is only *after marriage* that habitual faults [likely never even suspected before], sometimes come to the surface. Some couples give up in despair when they discover points of discord. They think their marriage must have been a mistake and their "beautiful dream" lies shattered. Sometimes they make no effort to build a stronger marriage together. There must be a determination on the part of both partners to make the marriage work. Potential life partners should not go into the marriage relationship with the idea that they can always get out of it if things don't work out.

When ripples surface between the two of you—always be quick to apologize and to ask forgiveness. [Jill], never be afraid to go to [John] and say, "I'm sorry I spoke so quickly; will you forgive me?" [John], never be too proud to go to [Jill] and say, "I'm sorry I hurt you; will you forgive me?" That is much more important than buying your partner a costly gift at Christmas time, or giving a $5.00 card on your anniversary. (You ought to give a card on her birthday and it is okay to buy a Christmas gift—but *learning to apologize and to forgive* is much more important than giving cards and buying gifts.) Every husband and wife needs to major on doing kind and helpful deeds, and practicing warmth and tenderness each day, even inside the walls of your house.

3. Live Within Your Financial Means

Most of us are caught up at times with the undue desire to gorge ourselves with trivial things. Jesus says, "Beware of covetousness, for one's life does not consist in the abundance of things he possesses" (Luke 12:15). In our materialistic age, it is easy to go head-over-heals into debt. It will be of tremendous help if you will observe the following tips:

a) It helps us to be good stewards of what God enables us to earn, and to be frugal and careful in our use of money, if we keep in mind:

--that 90% of the people on earth do not have an automobile

--that more people go to bed hungry each night, than there are people who have sufficient food

--that more mothers of the world see half of their offspring die in early childhood, than there are mothers who see their children reach maturity

--that more people live and die without the help of a single doctor, than there are people who have plenty of medical care

--and that while we search the refrigerator for an extra serving of dessert, many are searching daily to find just a bit of food in order to survive

b) Aside from the house in which you will live, make it a practice to never buy anything on credit. (The exception is, of course, if you *are absolutely sure* that you can pay the total amount at the end of the month when the bills come due—and you use a credit card merely for convenience.)

c) Never try and imitate your friends and neighbors in extravagant buying and lavish spending and unnecessary shopping trips. One writer says that the reason it is so hard for many of us to save money, is because our friends are always buying something we can't afford!

d) Remember that window-shopping is dangerous. Just looking in windows (or browsing through catalogs) for the fun of it, may be one way to spend an evening, but it is very easy for a person to convince himself that he must have what he sees. Window-shopping arouses new wants and triggers impulse buying.

e) Be slow about buying something because "It's a good deal." Getting something at a discount does not necessarily make it right or wise for us to buy the item. The statement, "It was such a good deal," or "I bought it on sale"—does not justify spending money for things that are not needed, or are not good and useful investments.

It is amazing, but understandable, that more than half of all marriage breakups start with squabbling over finances, budgets, and problems related to money.

The wife begins to work outside the home to help pay the bills—and when she works away from home—she gives her best hours and her best disposition to someone other than her husband and her children. In the evening she is tired, and frustrations can easily upset her—and as the years come and go, she loses a little bit of the close touch with her family.

The point of the message is this: live within your financial means; guard against frequent shopping and impulse buying; and make a commitment to be content with what the husband's income can buy.

4. Rule out the Possibility of Divorce

In recent decades, some churches and their pastors have held formal *divorce ceremonies* for those who think it is impossible for them to continue being married to each other. That is, they actually celebrate the break-up of two persons who have been married, whether for a short time or for many years, and invite persons to rejoice with them!

According to God's law, the marriage vows which two persons promise on the wedding day—before God and human witnesses, *may be broken only by death*. You promise to love and cherish each other *until death separates you*. Marriage is for a lifetime, not for a weekend.

Jesus says, as recorded in Mark 10:11-12 (Living Bible paraphrase), *"When a man divorces his wife to marry some-one else, he commits adultery against her; and if a wife divorces her husband and remarries, she too commits adultery."* The phrase "commits adultery" is in the present perfect tense, meaning that one who divorces and marries again while the original partner is still living, *keeps on* committing adultery—that is, lives in a state of adultery.

The pencil God uses to record a marriage has no eraser. The Bible gives no permission at any place or under any circumstance, for a divorced person to remarry.

One of the reasons why so many marriages are falling apart is related to the fact that couples often entertain the possibility of escape if things get rough. As a result, there is a loss of determination to stay married—but from God's point of view, marriage is a lifetime contract, and each couple must resolve to make the marriage work.

5. Observe the Rules of Common Sense

God has furnished human beings with a quality called "common sense." He expects us to use it. We have the ability to think, to weigh facts, to analyze situations—and the Lord expects us to use *our minds* to make worthwhile decisions. Here are some common sense suggestions related to marriage and family life.

a) Give God the first place in your home. The promise found in Matthew 6:33 is that if we give God first place, the necessities of life will be added unto us. Give God the first minutes of each day. *Have Bible reading and prayer each morning (or each evening) every day.* Give God the first day of the week. Use the Lord's Day for rest and worship and fellowship. Give God the first portion of your income, and be generous in supporting worthwhile causes. Give God's Son the first place in your heart. Live in light of His presence as the unseen Guest in your heart and home.

b) Determine to accept each other's personality traits unconditionally. No two persons will think alike about every issue that comes their way—no matter how similar their growing up experiences have been. Any attempt to compel your partner to conform to all of your personal preferences will tend to destroy harmony in your marriage. In courtship, differences often attract, but in marriage, differences can repel over the long haul.

c) Determine *who* in the marriage relationship will be responsible for what. Who will usually answer the phone? Who will write the checks? Who will shop for groceries?

d) Set up housekeeping away from your immediate families. Don't consider moving in with either of your parents, or even living next door to them.

e) Be prepared for dealing with a variety of crises in marriage. Marriage is for better *and for worse*. There are many crisis possibilities—severe illnesses, sudden accidents, financial reverses, disfigured children, etc. Keep spiritually fit so that you are ready to meet such trials with the confidence that God is with you.

f) Accept the fact that the sex relationship is not all that it is often talked up to be. Within marriage, it is a beautiful experience, and if you will observe the guidelines of decency and patience in this realm, and the information given in our private counseling—then the sex relationship will become a beautiful and enriching experience. It will help cement your love for each other into a binding relationship.

g) Learn how his mother prepares his favorite meals, and copy her recipes.

h) Plan activities which can be done together. Work on your financial budget together. Take a break from regular routine together. Visit historic and scenic places together. Attend meetings and fill obligations together.

i) Make a commitment to avoid correcting or criticizing each other in the presence of other people.

j) Maintain the spirit of courtship throughout your married days. Between the two of you, there should be words of encouragement and appreciation from time to time. [Jill], you can sometimes compliment [John] for his faithfulness to the job, for his ability to fix a leaking faucet, and for the time he spends reading to children. [John], you can sometimes compliment [Jill] for the way she cooks the meals and for her graciousness with guests. Your home should be a place (as the words of the song several decades ago said it), *"where seldom is heard a discouraging word."*

These have been components of a successful marriage. If you practice the guidelines we have just briefly examined, you can build a wonderful life together.

It is my prayer that *the sweetness* of courtship and *the glow* of romance, will never become lost when some of the routine duties of life and the trials of each day start crowding in. Those times will come, but please determine always to maintain the spirit of courtship.

Keep on writing notes to each other.

Keep on smiling into each other's face.

Keep on saying, "I love you."

Keep on going the second mile with each other.

Your friends believe that providentially God has brought you together, and we pray that He will blend your lives and unite your hearts to form one strong new family unit.

Chapter 4

THE ROLES OF HUSBAND, WIFE, AND CHILDREN

We look now at the responsibilities of the various members that constitute a family. A good family unit will have a dynamic leader for a father, a firm but warm-hearted mother, and cooperative children who respect both parents. Each member of the family has a part to play in making the home beautiful. Each has a God-given role (function) to perform. In God's order of things, the masculine role is that of being the breadwinner, and the feminine role is that of being a homemaker.

Preparation for the proper roles in the home usually begins in early childhood. A little girl is given dolls and dishes to play with in preparation for homemaking. A little boy receives toy trucks and tools in preparation for his role as breadwinner. If a child adopts the role of the opposite sex, he is termed a "sissy" and she becomes known as a "tomboy."

There is great confusion about proper roles in the home today—largely because of the efforts of the women's liberation movement, the influence of radical college professors, and the propaganda of the mass media. One state board of education, for example, forbids including in school textbooks, any pictures depicting women with aprons and vacuum cleaners.

The biblical roles, however, are quite clear. The husband is to exercise *loving leadership*; the wife is to manifest *quiet submission*; the children are to show *cooperative compliance*; and both parents are to concentrate day after day on *wholesome child training*.

1. The Husband—Loving Leadership

The husband is primarily to be a leader in the home. When a couple marries, the husband becomes the head of a new decision-making unit which we call "the family." The husband should set godly standards and lead the way by living up to those standards himself. He should lead off in family worship, prayer at mealtimes, and seeing that the family gets to church services at the proper times. The husband should enforce discipline in the home. He should try and make his wife's duties easier—by hanging up his clothes, coming for meals on time, and cleaning out his pockets before putting clothes in the wash hamper. The word "husband" means "house-band" and this implies that he is the one who should tie things together.

To perform the loving leadership role well, the husband should be diligent about cultivating at least three very important qualities.

a. He should be a faithful partner

All surveys indicate that many husbands have at some time or another been unfaithful to their wives. Satan has always tried to get people to believe that "the grass is greener on the other side of the fence"—and in the realm of human sexuality—the devil promotes the lie that sex relations with another woman would be a kind of paradise. Yet all studies indicate that a woman endowed with an unusually beautiful body is not necessarily a better sexual partner than one who is not so endowed.

From God's point of view it is an exceedingly wicked sin to be guilty of unfaithfulness to one's married partner—in any way, shape, or form. The sexual appetites within the human body have a powerful potential for misuse; our bodies can easily be aroused to lust. This is especially true for the male—and so all must constantly be on guard.

The husband can guard the tendency toward illicit lust *by avoiding* stimulating literature; *by concentrating* on his wife's good points (we tend to see the faults of those close to us and the virtues of those who are further removed); *by resolving* to live each day as if it were his last; and by *determining* to be loyal to the marriage vows (which include a promise to forsake all others and to love and honor and cherish the married partner until death separates the two). In Proverbs 5:20-21, God asks, "Why embrace the bosom of another man's wife? For a man's ways are in full view of the Lord, and he examines all his paths" (NIV).

b. He should be a diligent provider

In Proverbs 6:6-8, God reminds us of the tiny ant, and says, "Go to the ant...consider her ways and be wise; which, having no captain...provides her supplies in the summer and gathers her food in the harvest." The husband is to be a provider. "But if anyone does not provide for his own, and especially for those of his household, he has denied the faith and is worse than an unbeliever" (1 Timothy 5:8).

No matter how pious a man might appear to be on Sunday morning, if he does not seek to provide for the basic needs of his wife and family, he puts a bad light on the Christian faith. And so it is the husband's duty to work hard, to get to his place of employment on time, and to keep in mind the words of Scripture, "Whatever your hand finds to do, do it with your might" (Ecclesiastes 9:10). When God saves a man, He gives him a new love for his family, and he finds joy in providing for their needs even though every job has duties that are hard and routine and boring.

c. He should be a considerate companion

The husband's leadership role does not give him a license to become rude and to act like a selfish dictator. If we teach that a husband is to be "head" of the wife, we must equally stress that the husband is to love his wife even as his own body, and as Christ loved the church. Colossians 3:19 says it clearly: "Husbands, love your wives and do not be bitter toward them." And 1 Corinthians 7:3 says, "Let the husband render to his wife the affection due her."

The husband is to honor and respect his wife. He must seek to understand her. He must attempt to avoid those things that disturb her. He should hear the concerns of his wife, and listen to her advice, and be considerate of her feelings, and profit from her suggestions. It is only a matter of courtesy to appreciate her efforts and to be considerate of her feelings. Express appreciation for her cooking, her neatness of dress, her manner with the children, her gracious attitude toward guests, and the like.

Marriage is a precious relationship that needs much tender, self-sacrificing care. The Apostle Paul devotes twice as many words to telling husbands to love their wives, as he does to telling wives to submit to their husbands. A wife needs to be *told* by her husband that he loves her. Husbands, you can say it with flowers; you can say it with small gifts; you can say it by remembering anniversaries and birthdays; you can say it with the squeeze of a hand, with a vacuum cleaner, or a dish cloth; but above all say it with words!

Males and females are not identical physically and emotionally, in spite of all the attempts to equalize their roles today. The woman, in particular, needs to feel loved, needed, respected, and important to her husband. We husbands must be sensitive, understanding, and considerate; we must *tell* our wives that we love and appreciate them, and *show* them that we love them by doing the kinds of things mentioned above.

Sometimes a husband seems to enjoy making life hard and miserable for his partner. He becomes a kind of dictator who issues orders and his wife is expected to come running whenever he calls. If you are a husband who has been neglecting the duty of showing love, appreciation, and consideration to your spouse—go to your wife; apologize for your neglect; take out the family Bible; look over the record of your marriage; read some of the letters you wrote during courtship days; look at early pictures; bring home a box of candy to mark a special occasion; take your wife on a shopping trip; go along with her into the stores; take time out for a meal at a restaurant so that she is free from the chores of cooking the food and cleaning up the dishes.

The husband and wife both need to continue in the spirit of courtship throughout the years. If married couples worked as hard to *keep* each other as they once did to *catch* each other, most domestic home problems would be solved.

2. The Wife—Quiet Submission

The role of the wife is primarily that of homemaking. She is to be in a team-partnership with her husband, and the husband and wife should plan together, and discuss matters of concern together, but final decision-making on tough issues rests upon the husband's shoulders, and he must assume the responsibility for decisions made. There are at least three qualities the Christian wife should cultivate:

a. She should show proper submission

Just as a team needs a head coach, and a business needs a manager, so the home needs someone to be in charge. God says that the leader in the family situation is to be the man, and the wife should be submissive to her husband. Ephesians 5:22 says that wives are to submit to their husband's leadership in the same way that they submit to the Lord (LB).

The editor of a Lutheran magazine prepared a column each month in which he responded to readers' questions. He had been asked so often the question, "But why should males always be the leaders?"—that his reply in one edition of the magazine was this: *"Husbands are to be the leaders in the home simply because God decided that they should be! So stop asking!"*

The husband's role is no greater than the wife's. His role is not superior to hers; it is just different from hers. His leadership role relieves her of final decision-making. For example, an angry neighbor knocks on the front door and complains about damage the children did to his yard. The husband isn't home; the wife says, "I'll speak to my husband about it, and we'll take care of it." That is a proper response for the wife. She puts the responsibility on her husband. She doesn't need to make the decision. She is set free from the emotional burden of making final decisions, and taking the responsibility for them.

The wife should rejoice in her husband's authority over her. It is her special privilege to move day after day under the protection of his authority. This is women's liberation in a very real sense. Submission does not mean that the wife *should engage in sin* because her husband demands it.

All inter-personal relationships are to be governed by Acts 5:29, which says that we ought to obey God rather than human authorities. If a husband demands that his wife sign an income tax form that contains false statistics, or that his wife should lie about his whereabouts to protect him from state authorities—she need not obey. But the Christian wife should seek to comply with her husband's directives, even if his requests seem unwise or even unreasonable—unless such submission requires her to sin against God.

b. She should demonstrate kindly respect

The instruction from God's Word is found in Ephesians 5:33: "Let the wife see that she respects her husband." The Amplified Bible says, "Let the wife see that she respects her husband, notices him, regards him, honors him, venerates him, esteems him, and that she admires him exceedingly." The Christian wife must be careful not to say things that tend to injure him. She must not use sarcasm, bitterness, and verbal attacks. She must maintain a home that guards his respect and supports him.

Titus 2:4 says that the older women are to teach the younger women "to love their husbands." This means more than kissing him when he leaves for work in the morning. A wife can show love by acknowledging his headship in the home, by making no major decisions without his advice, and by keeping an orderly home.

Nothing breaks the spirit of a man more than a nagging wife. Readers may have heard about the man who went into a restaurant which had a huge sign overhead that read *Home Cooking*. The waitress said, "What can I get for you today, sir?" He said, "Do you have any cold beans?"

She said, "I think I can find some; anything else for you today?" He said, "Do you have any cornbread?"

"Sure. Is there anything else?"

He said, "Do you have any coffee made from grounds that are four or five days old?"

She said, "I think I can find some."

"Bring me a cup."

When the waitress finally had everything together, she said, "Anything else for you?" And the man responded by saying, "Would you sit at the other side of the table and nag at me—so I can really feel at home?"

Instead of nagging, try putting a love-note in your husband's coat pocket or his lunch bag. Find some way to tell him that you love him and that he is the most important human being in your life. If you don't show love for your husband, someone else most likely will.

The wife must never compare her husband's achievements with the accomplishments of another man. Wives, you *should not say* to your husband, "Look how nice Joe keeps his yard," or, "Dave often brings a gift home for his wife; why don't you do that?" Make it a point to try and express appreciation to your husband for a variety of things he does. Compliment him for his faithfulness on the job, his ability to open tight jar lids, or the time he spends playing with the children. Your home should not be a battleground, but a place where family members are encouraged.

c. She should major on tidy housekeeping

Many today are saying that housework and homemaking and motherhood are paths to misery. One feminist group ridicules homemaking, and says that "a housewife is an inhabitant of a domestic concentration camp."

The second chapter of Titus instructs the older women to teach the younger women how to conduct the affairs of home life. Older women are to "admonish the young women to love their husbands, to love their children, to be discreet, chaste, homemakers, good, obedient to their own husbands, that the word of God may not be blasphemed" (Titus 2:4-5).

The word *"homemakers"* (keepers at home/KJV) means literally "workers at home." Christian women should try to be *good housekeepers*, not seeking to be lavish, but tidy and neat. If there is anything that "turns most husbands off," it is a disordered house with nothing where it should be and everything where it should not be. The wife should work diligently at the task of trying to keep *the house* attractive and clean, and *the meals* tasty and well-prepared.

The word "homemakers" (or the phrase "keepers at home") means that the Christian woman should see that the home is her primary sphere of activity. It is best for younger women (mothers of small children) to be keepers at home, and not working at some job outside the home. There are some exceptions, but generally speaking, the father should be the breadwinner and the mother should be the homemaker.

There are special problems which are often associated with a mother's working outside the home, especially when there are small children in the family:

a) Children will be raised largely by baby-sitters.

b) There will be a tendency to alleviate guilt feelings by giving gifts to children to compensate for not giving them as much time.

c) There is sometimes the temptation to become too intimately involved with another man in the workplace.

d) It becomes easy to neglect personal devotions—Bible reading, meditation, and prayer.

e) Some develop an independent spirit, leading them to believe they can make it financially on their own, especially if there is a bad marriage.

f) The mother who works at a regular job outside the home gives her best hours and her best disposition to someone other than her husband and her children.

g) There are many additional expenses—extra clothes, baby sitting services, car and gasoline, higher income tax bracket, greater tension and thus medical bills, tendency to buy more than is really needed.

A child doesn't need wall-to-wall carpeting, beautiful drapes, a computer with internet access, and a new color television. Children need their mother's time and affection. Mothers should see their children off to school in the morning, and see them home again in the evening. Mothers should listen to their bedtime prayers and read to them from Bible story books. When children come home from school in the evening, bubbling over with concerns about things that have happened during the day, it is a tragedy if they must come home to the walls of an empty house.

The mother's primary ministry is to create a home which becomes a refuge for family members—a place to which they can come—away from the stress and turmoil of daily life. Each member of the family will go out to face the responsibilities of a new day better prepared because mother was there to organize, prepare, encourage, and pray.

3. Children—Cooperative Compliance

There are strong forces in our society which are pushing for "child rights"—the right to sue parents, to leave school when they please, and to handle their own finances. From God's point of view, there are at least three qualities to be cultivated by children with regard to their parents.

a. Children should show gratitude

The fifth of the Ten Commandments says, "Honor your father and your mother, that your days may be long upon the land which the Lord your God is giving you" (Exodus

20:12). The word "honor" means more than buying dad a new shirt on Father's Day; it means "to hold high in one's opinion; to respect another's place of authority."

Our parents cared for us, and provided for us, in the days and years when we could not provide for ourselves. If we had been left to ourselves, we would have perished. We must never forget the sacrifices our parents made for us—and so, regardless of who they are and what their accomplishments have been—we should honor and respect our parents, even if it is only out of gratitude for helping us survive the years when we were totally unable to help ourselves. When we hear a person speaking contemptuously of his dad or mother, we must recognize that here is an individual who has fallen very low indeed.

Many of us can be grateful that we were raised in a Christian home, brought up among God's people and in an atmosphere of soberness and of respect for life. In my own family there was poverty. We had our struggles during the depression years (the early 1930s). Mother washed on a scrub board; the roof leaked when it rained; there was no refrigerator. But the whole experience was a heritage for which I want to be eternally grateful. I want to say, "Thank you mother; thank you daddy," over and over again.

b. Children should practice obedience

The Bible clearly says, "Children, obey your parents in all things, for this is well pleasing to the Lord" (Colossians 3:20). Ephesians 6:1 says, "Children, obey your parents in the Lord, for this is right." The instruction in Ephesians 6 has no reference to the spiritual condition of the parents; rather, the reference is to the fact that *the Lord* places parents in *a position of authority* over children. The Phillips translation catches the essence of the thought: "Obey your parents whom God has set over you."

The Bible calls for total obedience on the part of children who have not yet left father and mother to establish a home of their own. (When a child marries and "cleaves" to his wife, the role of the parent changes from a correcting to a counseling responsibility. Genesis 2:24 indicates that a child "leaves" father and mother and "cleaves" to the married partner. The word "leaves" means "to abandon the former relationship." And so, after marriage, the parent *counsels* rather than *corrects* the child.)

God commands obedience for children because obedience is the path of safety. Danny was a seven-year-old boy with a big yard in which to play, but in winter he wanted to use his sled out on the road. One time when his mother saw him on the road, she called him and made him come inside and sit down, reminding him how she had told him never to sled on the road. Throughout the evening, Danny kept on asking to go out. He heard the laughter of others on the outside, and finally his mother let him go. As he went out the door, she said, "Remember what I told you Danny about going out on the street; you must stay in the yard." Those were the last words Danny ever heard his mother speak. Five minutes later he was killed on the road by an automobile.

Even teenagers should obey their parents and honestly try to abstain from what would offend them, even if they are not Christians. The father of a girl who was attending a revival meeting with some other girls, insisted that she stay home and do her school work. The girl was convinced that the services were important, and she really wanted to go, but her dad said "No." The next evening she asked the evangelist about it. She explained the situation, and he said, "Go home and obey your dad!"

The next night she stayed home and explained to her dad that the preacher told her to obey him and to stay home.

He said, "Did the preacher actually tell you to stay home?" She said, "The preacher said that the best way to please God and to be a good Christian is to be an obedient daughter." The father was deeply moved, and said, "If that's what you are hearing at church, you may go every night!"

Here again, Acts 5:29 applies. If parents teach a child to go out and steal, or to commit murder, the child must not obey his parents. Still—the child must demonstrate a Christ-like spirit. Children should treat their parents as they will wish they had treated them when they say their last "goodbye" to them—and as they *will wish* they had treated them when they lie cold and still in their caskets.

c. Children should give support to their parents

In 1 Timothy 5:4, the Bible teaches clearly that children and (or) grandchildren should "repay their parents." We need to help care for our parents in their old age.

The retirement home or nursing facility is not always the ideal solution. Many older people prefer to stay at home and be integrated with the family, rather than to be isolated away from the family in some small room in a home for the aging. Sometimes a nursing home is the only solution because the aged parent is so helpless that the family cannot physically handle the situation.

Some parents prefer a retirement community so as not to interrupt their children's schedules and privacy.

All of us have the responsibility of doing what we can to make the declining years of our parents as meaningful and as pleasant as possible. If we must feed our aging parents with a spoon, remember that they once fed us with a spoon. If we must help clothe them, remember that they helped to clothe us. If they drop food on the tablecloth, remember that we smeared the tablecloth sometimes too. We read about duties to widows and parents in 1 Timothy 5:4 (LB), *"But if they have children or grandchildren, these are the ones who should take the responsibility, for kindness should begin at home, supporting needy parents. This is something that pleases God very much."*

Our duty to parents includes a general spirit of gratitude toward them, obedience in childhood and youth, honor at all times, and giving support in their old age.

When others visit in your home, they should get a little idea of how the world should be run! The order, thrift, and discipline of the children—should be a miniature sample of what the whole community should be like here on earth.

In our homes, all parents have made mistakes. Mistakes call for repentance, confession, and forgiveness. We must never be afraid to go to our married partner and say, "I'm sorry; I was wrong; I spoke too quickly; will you forgive me?" Never be too proud to acknowledge your errors.

The family which takes seriously the Bible principles enumerated in the foregoing pages, and seeks to translate them into daily practice, will find joy and peace and beauty in living together. Your home will become a peaceful haven from the storms of life, and a school where great spiritual truths are learned. The hymn-writer says, *"There is beauty all around when there's love at home"*—and how true it is.

Chapter 5

THE NECESSITY FOR ADJUSTMENT
IN MARRIAGE

Wedded life is like the meeting of two rivers. I once stood in a high building in Belgrade, Yugoslavia and saw the meeting of the Sava and the Danube Rivers. The *Sava* begins in the high mountains of northern Yugoslavia. The *Danube* begins farther north in the continent of Europe. At Belgrade they meet.

At the point where the two rivers meet—at first there is turbulence, commotion, and there are lots of ripples. But in time, they blend and unite into one broad, peaceful stream, rolling on in majesty and strength without a trace of strife.

And so it often is when two independent lives (persons with differing habits and tastes and backgrounds) are first united into one. Sometimes there is a dashing of life against life—but with loving patience the two lives coalesce, and become a nobler, fuller, deeper, and richer harmonious unit.

Billy Graham says that the most difficult period of marriage is probably the first five years of adjustment.[2] Many couples would agree. It is during those years that we must learn to accept the faults of others.

1. The Need for Adjustment in Marriage

When the marriage ceremony is over and the privilege of establishing a home is begun, the problems of adjustment

---

[2] Graham says, "After about five years there develops an understanding so that a couple can communicate with each other without ever saying a word...I suppose it's been at least fifteen years since my wife and I have had a cross word between us. We think alike, believe alike, and desperately love each other. I love her far more now than I did when I married her" (*Billy Graham*, David Frost, 1997).

surface. It comes as a shock to couples, that their marriages must be worked at, hammered out, and prayed through. Two unique individuals must learn to mesh together in harmony.

There is great need for adjustment after the wedding simply because each partner is now a part of three families: the family in which you grew up; the family you marry into; the new family which your marriage establishes.

Marriage does not solve all problems; it usually creates some new ones. All of us are born with a certain degree of selfish independence. We come from different families, are brought up with differing expectations, and each has a unique personality structure.

a. Marriage partners' backgrounds differ

The more diverse the backgrounds, and the more differences we have in personality traits, the greater the number of adjustments that will be needed.

--the mother of one bakes pies that are sweet and cakes that are rich; the mother of the other bakes pies that are tart and cakes that are usually less rich.

--one family squeezes the middle of the tube of toothpaste; another carefully squeezes the end of the tube and rolls it up neatly as it is being used.

--some people like dogs and cats and lots of other critters around; others despise cat-hairs all over the sofa and the living room floor.

--some people are never comfortable when the temperature is under 75 degrees; others sweat easily and prefer the upper 60s.

--some people have a body metabolism that is slow in the morning and prefer to sleep in; others like to rise early and generally go to bed soon after dark. He likes to stay up late at night, and she is a morning person.

Living together 24 hours a day is far more demanding on each personality, than merely seeing each other for a few hours each week during the time of courtship.

Some advise that marriage is "a 50-50 proposition." I am not sure that is a correct statement. Sometimes we must all learn to "give and take"—but ideally, marriage (under God) should be "a 100-0 proposition." Each partner should go into the marriage experience with the commitment that he is going to give himself 100% to the purpose of making the marriage work, and she will make the same commitment. Each will seek to make the marriage partner happy, without expecting anything in return.

Too many persons enter into the marriage relationship without the determination to make the marriage work.

b) Marriage partners' temperaments differ

The word "temperament" is defined as "an individual's manner of thinking, behaving, or reacting to circumstances." There are four major kinds of human temperament.

Sanguine—warm, buoyant, lively

Choleric—active, practical, decisive

Melancholy—hesitant, shy, reluctant

Phlegmatic—calm, cool, slow, easy-going

Most persons are a mixture of temperaments, having characteristics of both parents, and of grandparents—but usually one temperament-type predominates in the individual life, with strains of one or two of the other types showing up.

1) *Sanguine*—expressive persons, warm, buoyant, and lively. Such individuals enjoy being with people; they like being surrounded by friends and seldom are at a loss for words. Sanguine persons are usually optimists. Sometimes

they lack depth and clear purpose in life. They talk long after a church service even when babies are tired and crying.

2) *Choleric*—persons who are called "drivers;" active, practical, decisive. They tend to be self-sufficient; they have a strong determination to succeed, and keep pushing ahead even when others become discouraged and quit. A husband's goal of wanting to succeed can cause his wife to feel neglected. They tend to be impulsive and fiery tempered. "Drivers" can easily become workaholics.

3) *Melancholy*—persons with analytical minds, hesitant, shy, reluctant. They do not easily make friends, must push themselves forward to make friends, but usually are very thorough and persistent once a decision is made. They are inclined to take life seriously; many melancholy persons are deep thinkers, artists, and scholars.

4) *Phlegmatic*—persons who are called "amiable." They are calm, cool, slow, and easy-going. For them, life seems to be a happy, pleasant experience. They seldom get ruffled or excited. They tend to be spectators and try not to get too in-volved. They are usually easy to live with, but their easy way of doing things can be a source of irritation to others. They sometimes lack motivation to get things done. They don't usually mind "sleeping in" in the morning. They are inclined to be a bit on the lazy side. Phlegmatic persons are willing to let others take the lead and make decisions.

Personality conflicts are usually temperament conflicts, and must be handled like other problems in life. When con-flicts arise remember certain basic principles:

1) Be open to genuine change. Just because your father or mother did some things in a certain way, does not mean that you must do those things in the same way.

2) Be quick to acknowledge wrong. Go to God, confess

your sin, and ask Him to give you a gracious spirit. Then confess your unkind behavior to your married partner so that your conscience is clear.

3) Be ready to respond with soft answers. It takes two people to argue. If you refuse to keep on disputing, especially quarreling with a raised voice—that ends the argument.

2. The Various Areas of Marital Adjustment

In this section we will look at the various areas where conflict often arises.

a. Problems with in-laws (domineering parents)

God ordained that newly-weds should separate from the parental families. Genesis 2:24 instructs the man to *leave* father and mother, and cleave to his wife. It is usually best for the newly married couple to start their own home away from both parents, even if they have to rent an apartment above somebody's garage for a start. My advice over the years has been this: It is good for the newly married couple to move far enough away so that the parents at least cannot see the chimney smoke!

Domineering parents can create problems for their married children. The mother (or mother-in-law) wants to tell the daughter (or daughter-in-law) what kinds of drapes to hang, what style of furniture to buy, where to place pictures and mottoes, and why she should change the kind of wash powder she uses and buy another brand. Sometimes parents find it terribly difficult to let go of their grown children, but that is a lesson that parents must learn.

On the wedding day the bride and groom become a new entity. Scripturally and morally they are no longer dependent children. The old relationship is changed. The young family should think of their parents as especially good friends, but parents must learn to move from a correcting to a counseling role. The young folks are free to accept advice from their parents, but they are not duty-bound to follow it.

There are special issues that certain families face. What about difficult stresses that arise if the son works on the family farm? What happens if the newly married couple is asked to provide a home for aging grandparents? It is the duty of children (or other relatives) to care for the older folks if that is what they sincerely want (1 Timothy 5:16), but if the family agrees to care for aging relatives, it is good to have a frank talk with them first. The husband can say something like this: "In our home, some things will be different; we will try to be fair to you; but in our home, I am the leader (the captain of the team), and what I say will be observed."

b. Sex adjustment (ignorance of biological facts)

Many couples discover that it takes a number of years to arrive at a mutually satisfactory sexual experience. Sex is not as glamorous as it is sometimes played up to be. The ideal and most satisfying fulfillment comes when both partners achieve orgasm at nearly the same time, but that often takes months or years to accomplish. Most couples expect too much from the sexual relationship.

The Bible teaches that one of the reasons for marriage is to enable married partners to fulfill each other's sexual needs, all within the context of a lifetime commitment. Sex within an honorable marriage is not sinful. Some seem to think that anything that is pleasurable is "bad"—like the little old lady who was given some ice cream for the first time. She tasted it, licked her lips, and said, "Why, it tastes so good it must be sinful!" But sex within marriage is not sinful.

Proverbs 5:18-19 says, *"Rejoice with the wife of your youth…let her breasts satisfy you at all times, and always be enraptured with her love."* First Corinthians 7:1-5 is the key New Testament passage on sex within marriage.

1) Verse 5—*Sex is a legitimate pleasure and is understood to be a regular activity* within a binding marriage. The phrase "come together again" recognizes the strong (but normal) sex drive in almost every human being.

2) Verse 2—*One of the purposes of marriage is to provide a wholesome release for the sex drive.* The Greek word for "fornication" (KJV) is *"pornia,"* which when used by itself speaks of all kinds of sexual immorality. Marriage is designed to help avoid temptation toward all kinds of sexual immorality—prostitution, incest, homosexuality, etc.

3) Verse 4—*Our sexual capacity does not exist for ourselves; it is provided for the benefit of our lawful partner.* Our bodies are not intended for self-manipulation (e.g. masturbation). Our sexuality is meant for communication; it is meant to be a gift for a lawful married partner. "The wife does not have authority [exclusive rights] over her own body…likewise the husband does not have authority over his own body, but the wife does."

All this must be understood within the framework of self-control. Self-control is one of the great virtues of the Christian life. It is a "fruit" of the Spirit—called *temperance* in the KJV (Galatians 5:23).

Sexual restraint within marriage is a normal part of life. Everyone who wants a good marriage must practice self-restraint. This includes restricting our eating habits, our use of the tongue, and our practices in the sexual relationship.

The virtue of self-restraint is related to birth control. God's standard for sexual activity is chastity before marriage and loyalty after marriage. Both require sexual restraint.

Many problems related to sexual adjustment are caused by ignorance regarding a few biological facts.

1) *The need for lovemaking (an arousal period) prior to intercourse (timing)*. Sexually, the male and female are timed differently. The man is aroused quickly, and as a result, most young men develop a hasty approach to having sex relations. He may become bold and crude, instead of being gentle and understanding and patient.

The woman is generally timed more slowly; sex feelings are often very meager at the beginning of the arousal period. As stimulation continues, pleasant sex feelings build up and develop—and rise higher and higher. It usually takes a longer time for the woman's arousal. As a result, some husbands tend to rape their partner. The husband must not expect his wife to turn on like a light bulb.

2) *The need for clitoral stimulation (distance)*. The clitoris is a tiny organ made up of many nerve endings which become the trigger that sets off orgasm in women. Husbands need to learn as much as they can from reliable Christian sources what it is that brings satisfaction for his wife. Good manuals include *"The Act of Marriage"* by Tim and Beverly LaHaye, and the book, *"Sexual Understanding In Marriage"* by Herbert J. Miles.

It is important to think seriously about birth control. The command to be fruitful and multiply, and replenish the earth (Genesis 1:28), in the English translation, sounds like a strict command to fill the earth by having as many children as possible. But the Hebrew construction of the text is really placing the emphasis *on the blessing that children bring*, not on the number of children that a woman can produce in a lifetime. As far as we know, Isaac and Rebecca (in Bible times) had only two children. In more recent times, Susanna Wesley gave birth to 19 children. Number 19 was a son named Charles Wesley—the writer of 6,000 hymns, some of which are among our favorites—including "A Charge to Keep I Have" and "Hark, the Herald Angels Sing." God has blessed both large and small families.

There is a natural way to basically control the size of a family. The "calendar rhythm method" is a natural God-given means of planning and spacing a family (birth control). It is based on the fact that a man's fertility is nearly constant day after day, but a woman's fertility is limited to a brief period during the time between menstrual cycles. The husband and wife must refrain from intercourse during the fertile period. The Christian virtue of self-restraint is required for natural contraception. There are good manuals that offer much help in this area. I recommend chapter 8 of the book entitled *"The Christian Couple"* by Larry and Nordis Christenson.

3) *The necessity for absolute privacy (concentration).* Privacy is especially important for the wife. It is hard to con- centrate on arousal when privacy is limited, or if there is no reasonable assurance that there will be no interruptions.

4) *The importance of careful bathing (cleanliness).* Any kind of offensive odor will tend to hinder the arousal activity which is so important to healthy sexual experiences.

There are a few practical concluding observations. First, couples must recognize that sex within the bonds of true and honorable marriage is good and sacred and God-blessed. Second, couples must not underestimate the importance of the arousal period. Third, couples cannot be quarrelling much of the day, and then expect the mood to be harmonious at night. One wife challenged the news columnist, Ann Landers with this statement: She said, "Most women view sex as

"Hold me close, and be tender; forget the act." Ann Landers asked her female reading audience what *they* think about that statement. Ninety thousand women responded—and 72% of the women who responded, agreed with the statement, "Forget the act; hold me close and be tender."

c. Controlling finances (danger of overspending)

God wants all of us to know that happiness does not come from having lots of money and lots of material things. Yet money is important, and we can't live in our society without it. See chapter 8 on managing money wisely.

The biggest problem in the area of finances is the temptation to over-spend. From the time we could crawl on our knees, we wanted a red wagon, and then a tricycle with a bell—and then a car and dozens of other things. In 1 Timothy 6:8 we are admonished to learn to live with less, and to be content with the basic necessities of life—food, clothing, and shelter.[3] Contentment does not come from having all our wants supplied, but from reducing our desires to include only the essentials of life!

A healthy balance toward material things is stated in Proverbs 30:8-9, which says, "Give me neither poverty nor riches…lest I be full and deny You…or lest I be poor and steal, and profane the name of my God." There are disadvantages to being desperately poor, *and* to being enormously rich. Our prayer should be, "Just give me sufficient for my normal needs." The simple Amish proverb is a wise saying: "Spend less than you earn and you will never be in debt."

If we live in luxury, dress in the height of fashion, buy

---

[3] "And having food and clothing, with these we shall be content." The word *clothing* is literally *coverings* (plural); it speaks of clothing to wear, and of a roof over our heads.

expensive hunting equipment, and get almost everything we want—where is the self denial? Where is crucifying the flesh? Where is our nonconformity to the world? Where is setting the affections on things above?

Some cautions about the use of money are repeated:

1) *Be careful about trying to keep up with others*. One writer says that the reason it's hard to save money, is that our neighbors are always buying something that we can't afford.

2) *Be aware that window shopping can be dangerous*. It often arouses new wants and triggers impulse buying. Avoid being lured into spending and buying by watching programs like the Home Shopping Network (HSN) on TV.

3) *Be slow about buying something because "it's a good deal."* Sometimes buying things at any price is not wise. The logic that "I bought it on a special sale" is nonsense. That does not justify spending money for things that we don't need or that are not a good investment.

It is important for God's people to avoid careless indulgence. Lots of families spend money to coordinate the furnishings and to match the colors of carpets and furniture and curtains—all of which is unnecessary.

I had a meal in the home of the principal of the Brethren High School in Bulsar, India (north of Bombay, in Gujarati State). The kitchen had a simple wooden table, several chairs, a lamp, a refrigerator, and an adequate meal of rice with some vegetables on top. There were none of the kitchen utensils such as we are accustomed to—but it was a delightful experience. It was the home of Nagalal Bulsari.

The advent of the super-market and the common use of the credit card, have had a tremendous impact on the buying habits of multitudes of people. The endless shopping sprees often lead to careless indulgence. Some American families are spending *more* each year than they earn—and down the road that will lead to disaster.

d. Facing inevitable changes (lack of mature faith)

Every family experiences changes that demand constant adjustment on the part of husband and wife.

--the life of a young child is snuffed out at an early age.

--the plant where the husband works has closed down.

--the death of the husband (and father) casts upon the wife the burden of keeping the family together, and providing a living for herself and the children.

--a long-term illness strikes a family member, and for several months (or years) members of the family need to make daily (or monthly) trips to doctors or to a hospital.

Sickness came to the home of Simon Peter's family (Mark 1:29-31), as it has to hundreds of homes since New Testament times. Some of the sicknesses are critical; others are less serious. Some family members do not recover; others regain their full health. Some of the illnesses come to people who are very devout in their service to Christ.

How do we cope with these changes? The answer: by developing a mature faith. There are at least three passages of Scripture that help in this area:

--*"all things work together for good to those who love God"* (Romans 8:28). One who believes this promise can walk after a casket out into the cemetery, and come back saying, "I know that God is in control and works things out for our welfare."

--*"before I was afflicted I went astray, but now I keep Your word"* (Psalm 119:67). Persons with a mature faith, ask, not "Why did this have to happen to me?" But, instead, "What do You want to teach me through this experience?"

--*"My grace is sufficient for you, for My strength is made perfect in weakness"* (2 Corinthians 12:9). A mature faith knows that weakness can lead to spiritual strength. We need strength to overthrow false ideas, to get along with other people, and to resist temptations firmly.

It is when we are at the end of the rope, and we don't know which way to turn, that the Lord often steps in, and in a special way, begins to conform us more and more into the kind of person that He wants us to become.[4]

3. How to Manage Quarrels between Spouses

Occasionally couples say that they have never quarreled, but it is really doubtful that two married partners ever lived together without some differences coming up between them. When conflicts and differences arise, try to talk about them.

a) Listen carefully; do not interrupt.

Allow the other partner to empty his or her heart, before you offer solutions. There are times to listen and not answer.

b) Communicate with calmness.

Do not allow yourself to explode emotionally, even if the other person does. Remember that "a soft answer turns away wrath, but a harsh word stirs up anger" (Proverbs 15:1).

c) Avoid making absolute statements.

Don't accuse with the words, "You're always worrying," or "You don't really love me," or "You're never composed."

d) Don't ever ridicule.

Nothing will estrange another person more than when he realizes that you are making fun of him.

---

[4] Another very encouraging thought can be gleaned from a comparison between Matthew 10:29 and Luke 12:6. Our eternal God is the God of the fifth sparrow. When four sparrows are sold, a fifth is thrown in for free—yet God notices that insignificant fifth sparrow. So He is concerned about us.

e) State your position clearly but charitably.

State the truth as you see it clearly but kindly (Ephesians 4:15). Speaking the truth is not enough; we must seek to speak the truth *in love*. Make the other person love you, not necessarily *for what you say*, but for *the way you say it*.

f) Accent the possibility of getting along harmoniously even though your views differ. The husband and wife and children don't all have to think alike about every detail, in order to live together harmoniously in the home. Mutual respect, especially for typical constitutional differences,[5] can heal relationships.

g) Foster a wholesome sense of humor. To have a sense of humor is a great asset in any human relationship. It acts as a shock-absorber to ease tensions. Marriage is a very serious matter, but there are many little incidents that occur each day—which, if you can laugh at them, can help avoid many tense situations.

God recognized the importance *of the adjustment stage* in marriage. Deuteronomy 24:5 says that when a man has taken a wife, he shall "be free at home one year, and bring happiness to his wife whom he has taken."

The newlyweds were not to be separated, nor was the husband to have any extra responsibility, so that the couple could make the necessary adjustments in their marriage. It is often wise also, for the couple to postpone the coming of their first child for a time, so that they don't have to assume the roles of mother and father, before they are accustomed to the roles of husband and wife. Natural birth control is not condemned in the Scriptures; instead, the Bible repeatedly emphasizes the need for temperance in all things.

---

[5]   Such differences include temperature settings, sleeping in late on Saturday mornings, deciding whether or not to have a bedtime snack, etc.

Chapter 6

PRACTICAL POINTERS FOR CHILD TRAINING

This chapter introduces three general principles related to biblical child training.

The 127th Psalm says, "Unless the Lord builds the house, they labor in vain who build it" (verse 1). This is a kind of general statement which says that no matter what our skills are, unless God helps us, we are going to fail. That concept is true in building a home and training children.

Psalm 127:3 says that children are a "reward." They are not a curse, a tragedy, an accident, or a nuisance. Children are an expression of God's favor. They are "a heritage from the Lord." Psalm 127:4 says they are like "arrows in the hand of a warrior." An arrow is a device intended to be launched toward a target. The target for a small child is to teach obedient and upright living.

If a group of people are out in a wooded area exploring its beauty, and a child strays from the party of people and gets lost, immediately they spread out over the hillside and search every spot hoping to find the child. The beauty of the woods doesn't seem so impressive any more. All attention now is focused on the search for a blue-eyed little girl— maybe less than two years old and perhaps weighing less than thirty pounds. But even though she is young, and still only very small—she is much more precious than all the vast bulk of mountain that was being admired only a few minutes before. The little girl is a human being. She can love and laugh and cry. She can sing and speak and pray. The mountain can not do those things. The child is a living soul, and therefore is a very precious possession.

Good homes don't just happen. They are the result of some careful planning and thought and discipline and prayer. It doesn't matter whether our house is a cabin on a hill, a cottage by the roadside, a farmhouse in the middle of an open field, or a mansion on the boulevard—it can either be a bit of heaven on earth or a bit of hell within four walls. It all depends on how faithfully we discharge our obligations.

Our homes are intended to become headquarters for the *spiritual training* of our children. There are at least three elements involved in the training of children, and the first of these is the need for diligent teaching.

1. Focus on Diligent Teaching

The families of Israel were commanded to teach the Word of God daily in their homes. The Bible says, "And these words which I command you today shall be in your heart, and you shall teach them diligently to your children, and shall talk of them when you sit in your house, when you walk by the way, when you lie down, and when you rise up" (Deuteronomy 6:6-7). This teaching is not to be an occasional or a sporadic thing. It is something to which we must give constant attention. There are many concepts related to diligent teaching.

a. Start early

Half of all growth in human intelligence takes place between the ages of one and four. During these early years, habits are formed and basic rules of life are learned. If you can't make a five-year-old pick up his toys, you probably will not be able to control him when he is fifteen. There is a critical period during the first five or six years of a child's life, when he can be taught proper attitudes, and if you miss the opportunity of those years, his openness to receiving instruction will likely never return. While there may be hope for a straying teenager through much persistence and prayer, it is much better to instill proper values into the lives of children at an early age.

b. Teach with love

The instruction of the Bible is, "Fathers, do not provoke your children [to anger], lest they become discouraged" (Colossians 3:21). This is an admonition against constantly nagging. Parents must discipline children, but parents must guard against nagging at children continually, lest they be made to feel they can't ever do anything right. The duty of the parent is not only to discipline, but also to bring encouragement. It is helpful to praise the child for a task well done whenever you can. Commend your daughter by saying, "You did a good job cleaning your room this morning." Or, say to your school-age son, "Your handwriting on that language paper was really well done." Most of us will bend over backwards to please someone who praises our efforts; we feel defeated in the presence of those who are frequently critical of us.

Another way to show children that we love them is to spend time with them. Don't merely do things *for* your children; do things *with* them. One father said, after spending an evening playing soft-ball with his children and with a few of the neighbor children (his muscles were aching and his back was sore), "I would sooner have a backache tonight than a heartache later on." That man was a wise father. Thousands of children get everything they want except their parents' time and attention. Don't pity the child who doesn't have a new bicycle, or whose parents cannot afford an encyclopedia. Rather, pity the child whose parents don't take time for a family picnic, or a walk in the woods, or a day at the zoo. Parents should have a regular play-time and a story-time with their children. Cultivate the art of spending time with your family.

c. Teach knowledge of the Bible

Training in the home is constantly taking place. Informally, everything we say, and how we say it; everything we do; everything we leave undone—all these things *are* teaching our children. Formally, one of the ways to teach our children by a planned and structured method, is to conduct brief regular daily family worship periods. Some of the most cherished memories of my childhood are the memories of those times when my parents would call us children together, and my father would get his Bible and read from its pages, and then we would kneel together for a brief period of prayer. These little worship periods only lasted five or six minutes, but they were diligently observed every day.

In too many homes, the things of the Lord are almost completely ignored during the week, even though the family may faithfully attend church services every Sunday. Parents must take time in the home to memorize Scriptures together, and to read good books to the children—and in this way plant a knowledge of the Bible (and of other wholesome literature) in the minds of children.

We found that memorizing Scriptures was made easier by choosing verses that begin with consecutive letters of the alphabet. For example, for the letter "a" one can use Proverbs 15:1 ("A soft answer turns away wrath, but a harsh word stirs up anger"), and for the letter "b" you can choose to memorize Ephesians 4:32, ("Be kind to one another, tenderhearted, forgiving one another, even as God in Christ forgave you"), etc. Write the verses on a large piece of heavy paper and go over them while gathered around the table for the evening meal.

Place them on small 3 x 5 cards and let each child have his own collection of memorized Bible verses. Small children like to collect bugs and leaves; why not encourage them to have their own collection of memorized Bible verses?

d) Teach immediate obedience

Obedience is the cornerstone of a child's future character. When you ask that something be done, there should be no questioning, no disputing, no answering back, and no delays. When you give a command, let your children know that it is going to be done—and if it is not done there will be immediate punishment. When mother and dad give a command, obedience is expected and required. Or, do your children know that you will repeat the command several times more if they don't respond? It is just as easy to teach a very young child to obey the first time as it is to get him to obey when told the ninth time—but you have to punish immediately, every time, if a child disobeys.

Some years ago one mother told her pastor this story, and all the while she seemed amused about the whole thing. She said, "Preacher, I have a six-year-old son, and you know, a funny thing happened the other day. He was out in the yard playing. I had his lunch ready; I had it nice and warm; and then I went out and called him and told him to come on in and eat his lunch."

"But," she said, "He never paid a bit of attention to me. I had to heat his lunch all over again. I warmed it a second time, and I called him again. I had to warm his lunch three times before he finally came in to eat."

The preacher said, "Lady, it doesn't take long to diagnose your case; you warmed the wrong thing. If you had warmed the right thing it would not have taken long for that boy and his lunch to get together."

One of the reasons why children *should not be* rotated from one baby-sitter to another is because there is usually no consistency with the discipline. Mothers of small children should be at home and constantly on the alert to see that the child obeys immediately.

e. Teach habits of work

Every child needs a planned routine of play and rest and work. They need jobs that are suited according to their ages and abilities. Girls should be taught household duties and there are plenty of chores that boys can do. From an early age, children can be taught to "make their own beds," and sweep up crumbs after a meal. There is nothing that challenges a young person more than to be given a responsibility. Assigned duties teach children that they are expected to take a job and to do it well.

To fail to teach our children the necessity of working, and to fail to assign them appropriate duties, is cruelty and not affection. Teach your children to work and let them know that money is not something that can be had for nothing.

Training children, then, involves diligent teaching. Begin early, do it with love, teach obedience, teach the Bible, teach habits of work.

2. Seek to Set a Godly Example

Another element involved in the proper training of children is good example. Instruction and teaching will not profit much unless it is backed up by the good example of our own lives. Titus 2:7 says that we should in all things show ourselves "a pattern of good works." A "pattern" is a model or guide for making things. We must live so that we can without

78

embarrassment ask our children to follow in the same path.

If a parent consistently drives an automobile over the speed limit, it is going to be hard to teach a child to respect the authorities of the government. Parents who divorce and re-marry are going to have a hard time persuading a child "not to break his word." A man who takes God's name in vain is go-ing to have a difficult time convincing his son not to swear. Dad and mother must live a life of integrity and respect if they expect their children to do likewise. Our children see our ways and they observe our behavior, and what they see has a much stronger affect on their minds than what they are told. They know whether or not we are phonies. They are better ob-servers of human behavior than we think they are.

If you pray often you will soon find your child imitating your prayers. If you attend church services on a regular basis, and without always being critical of the church, you can ex-pect your children to follow in attending church. If you gossip, your children will likely gossip too. When your child grows up, he is going to be pretty much like you. Children are great imitators. That is why English children have an English ac-cent, and Scottish children have a Scottish accent, and in the United States, southern children have a southern accent.

The father and mother who love and respect each other will be sending a message to their children—a message that they too are loved. Zig Ziglar tells a story about his family. He says that when his son was fifteen, *"I asked him what he would say to people if they asked him what he liked best about his dad?"* He paused only a moment before responding. The boy said, *"The thing I like best about my dad is that he loves my mom."*

When children see fathers and mothers loving each other, they feel much more secure and learn how to treat other people whom they meet. They will notice how you talk to each other.

They will notice whether dad opens doors for mother, or holds the chair while their mother is seated. Children learn from observing their mothers and fathers, and they try to imitate them. Most children would like to be the man or the woman their father and mother are.

There are little eyes upon you, and
They're watching night and day;
There are little ears that quickly
Take in every word you say.

You're the little fellow's idol,
You're the wisest of the wise;
In his little mind—about you
No suspicions ever rise.

You are setting an example,
Every day, in all that you do,
To the little boy who is waiting to
Grow up and become like you.

The task of training children involves not only teaching and instruction, but also the setting of a good example.

3. Pursue Consistent Discipline

A third element of training children involves consistent discipline. *Teaching* and *example* are not enough. There must be punishment for wrongdoing.

The child is born with a sinful nature. Every child is prone to do wrong, and almost constantly stands in need of correction. You can expect obedience if your children know that it is going to be required. *But if*, every time they whine and beg—you give in; *or if*, every time they weep and scream, you let them have their way; *or if* you give orders, and then never see that those orders are obeyed—your children will not learn obedience—and you will be to blame.

There is no one method of punishment that is always the best method. The natures of children are so different, that what might be a punishment for one, turns out to be no punishment at all for another. But we must certainly disagree with the modern notion that no child ought to ever be spanked. Some parents use bodily correction far too often, and much too viciously—but a good spanking not done in heated anger is still the best way to clear up a bitter attitude on the part of a rebellious child.

The Bible advocates firm discipline, and certainly the instruction is proper in Proverbs 19:18, when it says, "Chasten thy son while there is hope [while he is small], and let not thy soul spare for his crying" (KJV). And we are instructed further in Proverbs 13:24 with the words, "He who spares his rod hates his son, but he who loves him disciplines him promptly" [the marginal reference says *early*]. A child who learns respect for authority in the home will more quickly learn to respect the authority of God, and will more likely have proper respect for the authority of the state.

One teacher, teaching in a mid-western town, had two brilliant but unruly young fellows in her school classroom. The one was the son of a coal miner; the other, the son of a local politician. She took as much as she could from the unruly pair of boys, but one day she gave them both a good paddling. She says, "The coal miner father sent me a note the next day saying that I had done a good thing." She continues, "The other boy boasted that his dad would see to it that I didn't come back again the next year." The teacher had taught in the school system for twelve years, but the next year her contract was not renewed. She says, to make a long story short, "The *coal miner's son* later became a Senator in his home state; the *politician's son* (at the time of her writing) was serving a life-term in a federal penitentiary." The Bible says, "The rod and rebuke give wisdom, but a child left to himself brings shame to his mother" (Proverbs 29:15).

A child should not be given a spanking for everything. For example, if Walter is acting silly in the kitchen and he breaks an expensive dish, or he lets his dad's best saw out in the rain—this is often childish irresponsibility and it should be handled as such. Children don't act and think like adults. Children at different age levels have differing characteristics. The Apostle Paul says, "When I was a child, I spoke as a child, I understood as a child, I thought as a child" (1 Corinthians 13:11). There are childish ways of thinking, speaking, and reasoning—and parents must recognize this. Depending on his age and maturity, perhaps Walter should be made to pay for the loss, but a spanking should be reserved for these times when the child defiantly says, "No I won't" or "You keep quiet" or when he deliberately does something that he has been clearly told not to do.

If you have spanked in heated anger, or if you acted far too quickly, the best thing to do is to go to the child and apologize. Children will respect the authority of parents who are willing to admit that they have made mistakes.

There are several facts about using the paddle that need to be passed on to parents:

1) God has an ideal place prepared for spanking children. If they are spanked on the bottom, there is not much danger of permanent damage. By way of contrast, it is a real mistake to slap a child around the head.

2) It is a mistake to punish a child if he does not know

why he is being punished, or if he has not been warned in advance that certain actions will cause him to be spanked.

3) Never threaten a child with a spanking unless you mean it and fully intend to give him that spanking if he goes ahead and disobeys.

Children will usually test you out; they want to trust you; but if you make threats and then don't carry them out, they are confused. And parents must remember that *biblical spanking is not the same as social child abuse. Biblical spanking is punishment which is done with firmness, but always with careful moderation.* The parent who disciplines a child the biblical way will never injure or cause permanent damage to the child.

Some parents say that their children are so stubborn that it just doesn't do any good to spank them. I don't believe it. I don't believe there is a boy or girl anywhere that cannot be influenced by a good sound spanking—*if the parents begin early* enough, *if they are reasonable* with their demands, and *if mother and dad stand together and agree* that the punishment should be given. If you never punish your children you are doing them a grievous wrong. Good, firm, consistent discipline in your home will help your child repent sooner, behave better, live happier, and perhaps they will be delivered from Hell forever.

When a little child puts his small hand into yours—it might be smeared with chocolate ice cream; it might be grimy from petting a dog; the finger might be wrapped with a band aid. But the most important thing about those little hands is that they are the hands of the future. Those hands will someday either hold a Bible or else a deadly weapon. Those hands will either lead in church singing or spin a gambling wheel. Those hands will either dress a wound as a nurse in a hospital,

83

or tremble because they are controlled by an alcoholic mind. Thinking of a little child in these terms should challenge Christian parents to be as completely dedicated as possible to the task of training their children for God's glory. No sincere father or mother can look upon a child with all of his potential for sin and for going astray, and not tremble at the great responsibility.

There is a little prayer that should express the sincere desire of every true parent's heart. The unknown poet has used very moving words. The message says:

"Oh God, great Father, Lord and King,
Our children unto Thee we bring;
Guide their feet in holy ways;
Shine on them through darkest days.
Uphold them until their life be past,
And bring them safely into Heaven at last."

If you are a younger person who is reading this book, and you have never without reservation turned over your life to the Lord Jesus Christ, and have never set out to live by the standards of God's Word—it is important to be reminded that the greatest thing in life that any young person can do—is to remember his Creator in the days of his youth.

Give your heart to Jesus, while you are tender in years, before the winter of life sets in, and before your heart becomes cold and unproductive.

Don't go out into life alone. Take Jesus Christ with you. You will need Him as you face the trials of life.

Chapter 7

TEACHING CHILDREN THE VIRTUES
OF CHARACTER

The Christian home is to be more than a boarding house with a lunch counter. It is to be more than a place to eat and sleep and grumble and take a bath a few times each week. Our homes should become headquarters for the spiritual training of children.

Child-training is a large task. I do not claim to have all the answers, but I do speak from the vantage point of having some experience. My wife Priscilla, and I, have six children and twenty-seven grandchildren. Our aim in this chapter is to suggest ways to help children develop inner character, the qualities of faith, obedience, reverence, neatness, contentment, courtesy, and such virtues.

The message of the chapter is based on Bible truth, common sense, and practical experience.

1. The Quality of *Faith*

From a Christian perspective, *faith* is the firm conviction that the Bible is true, and that even things which are unseen by the natural eye are very real when stated in the Bible.

Hebrews 11:3 says, *"By faith we understand that the worlds were framed by the word of God, so that the things which are seen, were not made of things which are visible."*

Our children need faith to help them overcome the fears and uncertainties of life. We must plant in their minds an awareness of God's abiding presence and His constant help. We must lay the ground-work for faith. How do we do it?

a) Practice family worship at the beginning or the end of every day. The worship period should involve just a brief time of Bible reading and prayer.

Some of the most cherished memories of my childhood are the times when our family gathered each morning to worship God. When I think of the family altar, I am reminded of the poem: "Turn again, turn again, time in your flight; make me a child again just for tonight."

I will always carry with me a mental picture of a praying father and of family worship every day.

b) Consistently observe the first day of the week as the Lord's Day. Every day should be lived for the Lord, but keeping a special day—holy and free from unnecessary work, helps to cement the child's faith in God.

This is not to advocate that Sunday is to become restrictive or oppressive, and that we must sit stock-still in the corner of a room—but Sunday is not the time to be painting the house, mowing the lawn, tinkering with the car, or shopping at the Mall.

To observe the Lord's Day helps to keep a growing child conscious of the fact that we have a special concern about pleasing the living God.

c) Establish the practice of memorizing Scriptures together with the children. When children are still very small you can paste a picture on a large piece of cardboard, and write under the picture—a small part of a Bible verse. One of our favorites is the picture of a young boy on a wheelchair, with another little fellow bringing a kitten—for him to pet. And alongside the picture is the verse-portion, "Be kind." Children can learn that verse at a very early age.

As children grow older, we found it helpful to memorize together verses that begin with consecutive letters of the alphabet—for example, 1 John 3:23; Revelation 22:14; Matthew 11:28; etc. See the last paragraph on page 76.

The Bible should be given first place in the home. If we see that God's Son and God's Day and God's Word are given a special place of respect in the home—faith, in the hearts of our children, will be a growing and developing quality.

2. The Quality of *Obedience*

Obedience is the act of carrying out the instructions of another, that is, one who is in a position of authority.

Colossians 3:20 says, *"Children, obey your parents in all things, for this is well pleasing to the Lord."*

Teaching a child to obey quickly and quietly is one way to develop a child's character. We can gradually teach a child to become more and more obedient by doing several things. It will be a long process. It does not come overnight.

a) See that we ourselves (as parents) are obedient to those who are in authority. It must be our aim as parents to observe the speed laws when driving on the highway. We should not openly contradict the school teacher and stand up for the child. It is important not to violate the expectations of the church of which we are a part.

Parents who themselves disobey the laws of the land, and disrespect the authority of the teacher, and disregard the standards of the local church—cannot really expect their children to learn the quality of obedience.

b) Speak firmly and with a voice of authority, and mean what you say. Don't ask a small child a lot of questions. If we ask a small child whether he wants to do this or that, we are asking him a question that he doesn't know how to answer. His maturity level is often not ready to make wise decisions, plus such questions give the child an opportunity to display his authority—and sometimes he will say "No" to a suggestion simply to show that he is boss. As children get older they should be invited to participate in making decisions.

Don't ask your little daughter *if she wants to* take a nap this afternoon, or a young boy *if he wants to sweep up the crumbs* after the supper meal is finished. Don't give an order and then finish it with the question, "Okay?" For example, don't say, *"It's time to sweep up the crumbs, okay?"*

When a child is issued a command, and then the parent concludes the command with "Okay?"—he is asking the child if it is acceptable to him—if he really wants to obey!

c) Insist that your children obey each command without delay. Begin at the time of infancy, and teach respect for order, structure, and obedience—by feeding the child as much as possible at fairly regular intervals, and by following a regular daily schedule. Feeding a baby *on demand* implies that the baby knows best when it is time to be fed, and trains the child to be in control. Try to have a get-up time, a meal time, a play time, and a nap time.

As the child gets older, and he takes forbidden objects off the shelf, take him by the hand, and gently lead him back to the shelf, and explain that he must keep his hands off of those things. If the forbidden act is repeated, smack hard enough to give definite pain—and do it repeatedly until he remembers to obey.

Nadine Brown says, "I first thought that if I'd do that I'd be spanking our son every five minutes all day long!" "But," she says, "It didn't happen! Children are smarter than that. When our son realized that I was going to take up the switch and spank him each time—he paid attention to my orders."

It may take many punishments for several months, or even years. It may seem like your child will never learn, but he will—if you are consistent with the punishment.

The requirement to obey must be constant. The parent must be careful not to ignore even one single disobedience. That's why frequently letting children with a baby-sitter is not a wise thing to do. By the time children are six or eight years old, they will automatically obey—if they are trained to obey during the early years. See also page 77 in this book.

What are some appropriate punishments when a child disobeys? We found that differing punishments for children at different age levels seem appropriate:

Ages 1-3 (very small children)—smack the hands.

Ages 3-9 (when they are older)—use the paddle.

Ages 10-up (when still older)—withhold privileges.

If there is harmony between husband and wife, they can stand together in discipline. See pages 82-83 in this book for more instructions related to disciplining a child.

It seems easier for some parents just to let things slide and to let children go unchallenged—than to enforce rules. I can't think of anything that parents could do to children *more heartless* than failing to discipline. Elisabeth Elliot[6] says that if she was given a command "and *then* did not budge, Mother resorted to what she called 'the speedy application of a switch to little legs.' The switch was a thin stick about eighteen inches long, one of which she kept above the door in every room of the house."

It is a fact that those children whose wills are trained to

---

[6] *The Shaping of a Christian Family*, page 134.

89

obey are more free, more happy, and more pleasant to be around, than those who repeatedly get their own way.

There are a number of reasons why parents neglect the discipline of obedience. For some parents, the neglect is due to ignorance regarding the corruption of depravity in each child. Others fail to insist on obedience because they think the children will not love them. Yet Hebrews 12:9 says that we "have had human fathers who corrected us, and we paid them respect." Some parents are lenient toward their children because they believe that "children will be children, and that they will simply be disobedient until they grow up."

3. The Quality of *Gratitude*

Thankfulness is an important attitude; It is a warm feeling of appreciation for the benefits we have received from another. Children should be taught *to always express thanks* when someone does a favor for them. If they receive gifts from friends or relatives who live at a distance, children should be diligent about sending "Thank you" notes.

Ephesians 5:20 says that we should give *"thanks always for all things, to God the Father, in the name of our Lord Jesus Christ."* Thankfulness is related to *contentment*, and contentment is the quality of being happy enough with what one has—without demanding more and more. Those who are content with meager belongings, tend to be more thankful than those who are deluged with plenty.

In our day of material abundance, the art of showing gratitude is often neglected. We can teach children to be grateful by teaching the virtue of contentment. Children must be reminded frequently to be thankful for the gifts and the benefits they receive. There are several principles to keep in mind when encouraging contentment.

a) Determine to live a life that is simple in taste and style. Don't let a child become accustomed to the choicest food, a big variety of clothes, and lavish birthday gifts.

Children should be taught, on occasion, to amuse themselves with ordinary things such as *spools*, *clothes pins*, *popsickle sticks*, and *cardboard boxes*. Children love to play with an empty box. They throw it around, hide behind it, crawl into it, and use it for a house. Have you ever seen a child get a $30 toy, and spend more time playing with the *box* it came in—than playing with the toy itself?

We found that it is good not to let toy catalogs and newspaper advertisements lying around the house for children to see. It usually breeds dissatisfaction. They think they must have what they see.

We must resist the urge to buy lots of toys and other consumer goods that are not really useful or necessary. Be careful at Christmas time—even if you have the money.

b) Insist that children eat what is served to them, or go hungry. Children should be served only small amounts of food at a time—and then, if still hungry, they should be served another small amount, so that none goes wasted.

Food can be simple and still tasty. Let children learn to be satisfied on occasion with a peanut-butter-and-jelly sandwich, rather than thinking they must have ham and cheese on a croissant roll. It certainly cannot be right for us to overeat, or to throw good food away, when a significant number of people go to bed hungry at night.

c) Stress the Bible teaching on giving, by exposing your children to the needs of those who are less fortunate. The opposite of contentment is greed—a lust for more and more things. But God has a remedy. The great Christian antidote for the poison of greed is the grace of giving. As soon as children receive an income they should be taught to give a portion to the Lord's work. And under grace, we should voluntarily give generously to expand the Lord's work.

During the depression years of the 1930s we were very poor. Mother did not have a washing machine, or an indoor toilet, and not even a drain in her sink. A number of men would try and eke out a living by selling spools of thread and other small household items. They were called "tramps," and often mother would give them a meal.

One family on a trip recently stopped at a fast-food restaurant for a quick breakfast. There was a homeless man outside the Burger King who asked them for money to buy some food. The parents were first inclined not to give the money, but the father says, "Thankfully, we did." He says, "Our little 4-year-old talked about it during the entire trip, and she still on occasions mentions it."

By teaching children to give to others, we are helping them overcome the sins of covetousness and greed. Teach children that getting money involves hard work and controlled spending.

d) Take your children to visit a junkyard or a city dump in your community. Nothing impresses an individual with the emptiness of material goods—like a trip to a junkyard or a dump. Take a look at everything in those places, and keep in mind that *all of it* was once someone's treasure.

One of our grandsons has found a number of snowmobiles on the city dump. He retrieves them, repairs them, paints them, and sells them.

Helping our children to develop thankful hearts is an ongoing process. Those who have gardens know that a beautiful garden doesn't pop up overnight. Seeds are planted, and watered long before any fruit comes as a result of the labor. That's how it is with child-training.

4. The Quality of *Courtesy*

Courtesy is the act of being gracious and helpful and polite, even in small things.

The Lord expects all of us to practice good social manners—to say "Thank you" and "Please"—even to members of our own families. If children are not taught good manners, they will run in the house, grab for the biggest apple, and interrupt when others are talking—because (like all of us) they've been born with selfish tendencies, and so they have to be *taught* proper behavior.

a) Try always to be consistent in your own practice of good manners. Parents must themselves strive to practice courtesy toward other people on every occasion.

We must be careful not to be courteous only toward certain people in respected positions of authority, but toward all persons—even those who may be somewhat feeble and less renowned in this world—courteous to old people, crippled people, odd people, black people, Oriental people, simple people, and so forth.

b) Constantly encourage deliberate acts of thoughtfulness toward others. We must teach children not only to say "Please" and "Thank you." (Those expressions are proper, but they can easily become meaningless and routine phrases.)

Children must be *taught* to, on occasion, *give* a toy to another who is less privileged; to let another child have first turn because he is a guest; to keep especially calm and quiet when someone is ill, or resting.

c) Determine not to allow any kind of "name-calling." Courtesy to all persons means that we avoid calling people names like "dummy" or "stupid" or "dodo" or "dingbat"—or whatever is currently the ugly name to use.

In the Bible, we have an account of some children who were name-calling, mocking a middle-aged man, and calling him a "baldhead." This lack of courtesy was so offensive to the God of heaven, that the Lord himself intervened. God let a couple of bears come rushing out of the woods, and they mangled the bodies of 42 children. That account is given in 2 Kings 2:23-24.

The next time any of us is tempted to make derisive fun of other people, we had better remember what God thinks of those who laugh in scorn at others.

Parents need to do their best to teach children to answer questions when greeted by a visitor. Children must learn to speak to others with courtesy.

I was scheduled to speak in the Bakersfield, CA Church of the Brethren, and when my wife and I arrived at the pastor's home we were received graciously. Soon after our arrival, their three children came home from school and each one greeted us warmly. The oldest boy (about ten years of age) came in the door, walked over to us, and said, "We feel honored that you came to our home."

In some homes when a child appears, and the guest says "Hello"—he doesn't even get a grunt in return. It is true that children differ; some are more outgoing than others, but when someone doesn't respond to a greeting, it implies that the person who is speaking is not worthy of a response.

Parents should try and see that children stop what they are doing and listen carefully when they are spoken to by another, and respond to each greeting. We are respect older persons and rise before the gray headed (Leviticus 19:32).

Have you ever taken an elevator down to the first floor, and been unable to exit, because as soon as the door has begun to open—children have started piling in so fast that you can hardly get off? Sometimes those youth are teen-agers, and their parents are standing right behind them, but they say nothing by way of correction.

Teach your children elevator etiquette! The Scriptures say that we are to have compassion for one another, love as brothers, and we are to *"be tenderhearted [and] be court-eous"* to one another (1 Peter 3:8).

5. The Quality of *Neatness*

Neatness is the quality of keeping things clean and trim and tidy and precise. Modern art and poetry often stress the confusion and disorder of the times in which we live. Obser-vers often can't tell whether the painting represents a sunset or scrambled eggs! Vance Havner once visited an art display where a particular painting won first prize, only to learn later that the maintenance people had hung it upside down.

In earlier times there was a simple poem that taught respect for order:

"One, two—buckle my shoe;
Three, four—shut the door;
Five, six—pick up sticks;
Seven, eight—lay them straight"

The poem teaches that buckling a shoe is better than letting it unbuckled. The door is orderly when it is shut; the scattered sticks should be picked up and laid straight.

How does one teach neatness?

a) Parents should teach neatness, cleanliness, and order at a young age. Establish routines for getting up in the morning, for meal times, for work times, for story times, and for bed-time. Children will feel more secure if things are done the same way day after day and week after week.

Some parents make the mistake of purposely not cleaning a small child's diaper for a long time. They say, "Maybe he will get tired of it and the next time will ask for the potty." But what such action does is train the child to be comfortable in a "mess." Some children feel comfortable in clutter and dirt and disorder. They've been trained that way.

b) Parents should keep the house tidy and in order. It is a good practice not to go away from home unless the table is cleaned off, toys are picked up, and the crumbs are swept off the floor. Things ought to be clean, and in their proper place, before the family goes to bed at night.

Children should always be taught not to come into the house with muddy boots; not to throw peanut shells on the floor; not to rub over the window glass with their fingers and hands. Youth should keep their rooms in neat shape.

c) Children must keep their bedroom orderly and clean. The child's bedroom is an important place in his early life. It is here where he closes his eyes on the scenes of the day, and it is here where his eyes open to behold another new day. The bedroom should not be so disordered that the child has to start the day with a depressed feeling.

Clothes should be hung in their proper places.

Beds should be made.

Books should be arranged neatly and in order.

God is a God of neatness and order; He does not expect our homes to have the appearance of chaos.

Young women should be taught to be good "home-makers" (Titus 2:5). Some emphasize the word "home," but the emphasis must also be on "makers." Mothers are to be good workers and neat housekeepers.

6. The Quality of *Reverence*

Reverence is a feeling of deep respect—a sense of awe for that which is sacred.

Proverbs 1:7 says, *"The fear of the Lord (that is, reverence for holy things) is the beginning of...wisdom."*

There are practical ways by which parents can teach respect for that which is sacred and holy.

a) Children must be taught reverence in the church service. The child needs to learn that in certain places he is to be quiet. One of the best ways to teach a child to sit quietly in church services, is to make him sit quietly during the family worship times in the home. There is no better school-room for teaching reverence in the church service, than at family worship time in the home.

If he refuses to sit silently during family worship, smack the hands hard enough to cause discomfort, and eventually the child will likely associate Bible reading and prayer with times when we must sit quietly.

If the child persists in crying too loudly (or otherwise misbehaving) during a church service—take him out; hold him tightly; don't let him walk around. He must learn that it is less fun to be taken out than it is to stay in the service. If taken out, don't give the child any toys or anything to eat.

Parents should be sure to have children stay with them

after the service, or with a responsible person. It is sacrilegious to let your children run around in the church building after the service, as if they were a gang of Apache Indians chasing an enemy.

b) Children should be taught reverence in the home setting. Each parent must carefully show respect for the other. If there are occasional lapses of respect between mother and dad, apologies should be made to each other.

Children, by noting such action, will learn that parents are human too—and they respect the honesty and humility of those who are willing to apologize.

Reverence in the home setting will include *restricting* the kinds of music children listen to, the kinds of programs they hear on the radio, the kinds of sites they view on the internet or on television, and the kinds of toys they play with day after day. Reverence for things sacred in the home can be amplified by being careful about the kinds of dress parents allow their children to wear.

For example, the toys we buy for our children send messages to them about those values that we consider to be important. Parents must choose toys that are consistent with the values and the character qualities they are trying to teach the children.

If little girls are part of the family, they may have baby dolls to play with, but surely not the leggy, busty movie-star dolls. They represent the kinds of people you don't want your daughters to emulate. And now, in the first decade of the twenty-first century, the "Barbie Dolls" are being replaced with an even more offensive group of dolls known as the "Bratz" line. It makes no sense to establish one set of values regarding dress and lifestyle, and yet permit children to interact daily with a toy that represents the opposite.

And for young boys—have you seen the many toys which are replicas of ugly military equipment? Parents should teach their children to play with puzzles and tools rather than with toy guns. Why teach little boys to use and play with equipment that represents disrespect for human life? Such toys hardly represent the things that are "lovely" and of "good report" (Philippians 4:8).

c) Children should be taught reverence for God's handiwork in nature. Take time to point out to your children:

The beauty of an unfolding flower

The strength of a giant tree in a storm

The variety of birds that come to the feeder

Talking about God's greatness and goodness is not something we do only on Sundays, and in a church service.

I will never forget coming in from our large garden, on warm summer evenings, seventy years ago when I was a boy. We worked until dark, and then on clear summer evenings my dad would lie on his back, on the grass, and would point out the Big Dipper, the Milky Way, the North Star, and some of the constellations. Then he would sometimes recite the little poem—"Twinkle, twinkle little star, how I wonder where you are!"

The fear of the Lord (a sense of reverence for God) is the beginning of wisdom.

7. The Quality of *Truthfulness*

Truthfulness is the art of accurately reporting facts and events. It includes the concepts of being *loyal* and *genuine* and *honest*.

The Bible says, "All liars shall have their part in the lake which burns with fire" (Rev. 21:8), and at another place, "Lying lips are an abomination to the Lord, but those who deal truthfully are His delight" (Proverbs 12:22).

For the most part, truthfulness is a vanished virtue in our day, especially in Western society where being noted for telling the truth was once an important virtue.

We must never assume that our children couldn't tell an untruth. Some parents will say, "But I know that my son [or my daughter] would never tell a bare-faced lie!"

The fact is—every child has the potential to deceive, and so we must teach children *to admit* wrong, and if needful, *to apologize* to any person he/she has wronged. There are some things to keep in mind when trying to encourage truthfulness:

a) Parents must avoid any type of deception.

A well-dressed mother walked into a large grocery store, went to the produce department, and looked around carefully. When she thought that no one was watching, she dumped three boxes of strawberries on a table, picked out the choice berries, and placed them in one box. She put that box in her shopping cart and placed the other two boxes back on display. Parents must themselves be an example of truth-fulness. The mother paid for the berries, but she was being deceptive, and was cheating other customers. Parents must be careful never to practice even mild dishonesty.

b) Parents must not permit exaggeration in speech.

There are certain expressions that are borderline figures of speech:

"I was scared to death"
"Thanks a million"
"I nearly died laughing"

A child who was brought up in that kind of atmosphere, came home from the zoo, and said, *"Mommy, the giraffe had a neck a mile long!"* The mother said, "Haven't I told you a thousand times never to exaggerate!"

I know, *we don't mean anything* by these expressions—but that's just the point. Jesus says that *we should avoid* every idle word—that is, we should avoid all those words and expressions which mean nothing!

c) Parents must avoid undue scrupulousness about fine points.

We should not worry over having said, "It is ten past two"—when, in fact, it was only eight past two."

It is very important that we don't get caught up in promoting the "Santa Claus myth"—or in thinking that it's okay to deceive another persons if we are trying to pull a surprise on him/her. Children will believe that Santa is real, and then later discover that they have been deceived.

God says that he who practices "deceit shall not dwell within my house; he who ["speaks falsely" NIV] shall not continue in my presence" (Psalm 101:7).

It may be helpful *to reduce punishment* for offenses when the child tells the truth immediately and completely. It can also be helpful to tell stories from the life of Abraham Lincoln—examples of his careful honesty as a youth and his integrity as a store-keeper in New Salem, Illinois.

8. The Quality of *Diligence*

Every child needs to learn the lessons of diligence. Diligence refers to painstaking *perseverance* at one's work and study; it refers to one who sticks it out; the quality of finishing a task that is assigned.

a) We must teach children to keep on trying.

Teach children the lesson implied by the proverb, *"If at first you don't succeed, try, try again."*

If your son can't beat you in checkers, don't deliberately make a blunder to let him win; rather, tell him how to play so that he can win by himself!

If a small child can't make what he wants with his blocks, encourage him to try again. Get down on the floor with him and help him a little bit.

Let a small child play most of the time, but as children get older, they should be assigned work along with play—and should know that the work must always be done, even though it will sometimes seem monotonous.

b) Do not tolerate sloppiness in work.

Many people tend to be sloppy in their work. All human beings are given to a certain amount of laziness.

Children need to learn that laziness leads to a lot of inconvenience. If you don't believe it, try spending just one day when everyone in the family does nothing—including mother! See what happens.

On occasion it may help to let children make some choices, and then require them to live by the results of those choices.

Many families expect their children to help with the work of maintaining a large garden. If a child complains about *not wanting to help* pull weeds or pick strawberries— give him the freedom to quit and to go play. But remind the child that when the family sits down for supper, he will have to go hungry. The choice is his—and that procedure is supported in the Bible (2 Thessalonians 3:10).

c) Set limits with loss of rewards when late.

Sometimes children have the habit of dawdling—to piddle around and waste time. They fritter away long periods of time to do a job that should only take a few minutes.

Probably the best approach for this problem is to set time limits, and bring punishment if the child is late with completing the task. Help children understand that diligence is much more enjoyable than is slothfulness.

Teach children to get a job done, and then go on with the day!

Most children love to help dad and mother. They think it is fun to sweep and dust and set the table and dry the dishes. Having them help, even though it takes longer, will pay dividends later.

But the time will come when the novelty wears off and they will no longer think it is fun!

Then the parent needs to firmly insist on performing their chores as a normal routine.

In too many homes, the children are free-loading guests. They consume food, relax in bed, and enjoy entertainment while the parents do the work.

The results lead to irresponsibility, selfishness, and laziness. These are not qualities which become good advertisements for the Christian faith.

Understanding human behavior is one of the keys to effective child training—and the first basic concept is that each individual person genetically receives a depraved self-centered nature at the time of birth.

God's analysis of human character is not very flattering. God says that "All we like sheep have gone astray; we have turned every one to his own way" (Isaiah 53:6).

Regardless of whether our background is Christian or pagan—*we have all been born* with sinful natures *that are far worse* than most of us are willing to admit. We *are inclined to do wrong* to a *far greater degree* than most of us would like to say.

Children are not innocent little darlings, thinking only angelic thoughts. The child is not innately "good." Psalm 51:5 says, *"Surely I was sinful...from the time my mother conceived me"* (NIV). Psalm 58:3 says, *"They go astray as soon as they are born."* A child if left to himself will choose a wicked and shameful lifestyle. Proverbs 29:15 declares that *"A child left to himself brings shame to his mother."*

Ingrained in the nature of every child is a persistent determination to manage his own life independently of any authority. Even a small child is very self-centered; he believes that all things exist *for* him and *because of* him.

Raising courteous and well-disciplined children requires patience, common sense, and a lot of God's grace. Coddling children and spoiling them—giving in to their whining and wants, *may seem to be* a form of love—but that is not love; it is *the mark of a lazy parent*.

The responsibility of training children is a difficult one. Sometimes it is very frustrating—and you will wonder whether your children will ever match your goals for them, but keep on working at character building—it will pay rich dividends, and someday your children will rise up and call you blessed. Every parent needs to be constantly committed to teaching good character traits.

Chapter 8

POINTERS ON WISELY MANAGING MONEY

As Christians, we have been taught fairly often about *giving* generously to worthy causes, but sometimes not much is said about how to faithfully handle the money we spend for our necessary family needs. God is not only concerned with the amount we give to support various Christian ministries; He is also concerned about how we use our *entire* income.

I was born in 1930. The Great Depression in the United States came in October, 1929. Money was very scarce in those days. My mother washed clothes on a scrubboard. We had no indoor plumbing, no bathroom, not even a drain in our kitchen sink.

I never rode a school bus; we walked or rode a bicycle to school. Every Wednesday my sisters and I were each given one penny to buy candy on our way home from school. Our food was mashed potatoes, baked beans, peanut butter crackers, mush and milk, and fried mush the next morning. We had vegetables and fruits during the summer growing season, and that was largely our diet. We generally had meat at meal-times only on those Sundays when we had company for the noon meal. I worked during the summer (in early teen years) picking up potatoes for 50 cents a day –and in a hardware store (in mid-teen years) for 16 cents an hour—and while in college, I worked for a plumber (in the office) for 40 cents an hour.

But actually, I had it pretty good compared to the masses of people who inhabit the earth. We learn to read, and go to doctors, and eat nutritious foods—but millions of refugees in Pakistan, Mozambique, and Sudan live day after day on fruits and nuts, and on broth made by boiling tree roots. More people on earth have a life-span of *less than* 45 years, than there are people who have a life-span of at least threescore and ten. We feel handicapped without electricity for two hours, but many people in the world will never have access to electricity, not even for five minutes!

The major point of the lesson is that, as Christians, we are to be *thrifty* without being *miserly*.

1. Principles of Good Money Management

There are some basic principles that should govern our use of money.

a. Acknowledge God's ownership.

(Psalm 24:1) "The earth is the Lord's and all its full-ness; the world and those who dwell therein."

All that we are and all that we have—belongs to God. God owns everything; we are stewards of that which belongs to God—and a steward is to be a faithful caretaker of that which belongs to another. We don't own anything. All that we have is on loan, and God holds the note. When we check out of this life and go into the next—there's going to be a final accounting.

b. Avoid careless indulgence.

(1 Timothy 6:8) "And having food and clothing, with these we shall be content."

Lots of families spend money to coordinate the fur-nishings—to match the colors of carpets and furniture and curtains, all of which seems unnecessary.

It seems obvious that the advent of the supermarket and the common use of the credit card have had a tremendous impact on the buying habits of multitudes of people. The endless shopping sprees often lead to careless indulgence. Some American families are spending *more* each year than they earn—and that, down the road, will lead to disaster.

c. Prepare for unexpected decreases.

(Philippians 4:12) "I know how to be abased, and I know how to abound [speaking of money]...I have learned both...to abound and to suffer need."

We must be alert to the fact that our income could be reduced because of an economic slowdown, a physical injury, a company's change of hands, a fire that burns a property, or a death in the family.

The best preparation for any possible future financial stress, is to try and stay out of debt, share generously with others, and trust God for His provision even in hard times.

d. Have peace about your purchases.

(Colossians 3:15) "Let the peace of God rule (be an umpire) in your hearts."

This means that most spur-of-the-moment decisions to buy—should be avoided. Jesus says that when we contemplate buying (or building), we should sit down first and count the cost (Luke 14:28).

Each time we have an urge to spend for another item, it is a good idea to put it on an "impulse list"—date it, wait 30 days, pray about it, and then see if you still want to buy it. Most people who do that generally only buy about half of what they earlier wanted. (If you are considering buying a lemon at the grocery store, I doubt that you should struggle over such a purchase.)

e. Consider your witness to others.

(1 Corinthians 10:31) "Therefore, whether you eat or drink, or whatever you do, do all to the glory of God."

We should avoid extravagance in our daily living, for if we live in luxury and dress in the very best garments, where is the self-denial? Where is overcoming the flesh? Where is nonconformity to the world? Where is setting our affections on things above?

Certainly, having closets full of clothes *that are seldom used*, and living a lifestyle *characterized by undisciplined spending and luxury*—is a mistake for God's people. Most people would likely do well to take steps toward simplifying their living standards.

2. Bible Teachings on Attitudes to Avoid

Every Christian has probably read that it is easier for a camel to go through the eye of a needle, than for a rich person to enter the kingdom of God (Luke 18:25). Yet many find it easy to pursue more and more wealth, instead of striving to live on less.

Money is one of the most unsatisfying of possessions. Having wealth *does* take away some cares, but it brings with it many additional concerns. One writer says about money: *"There is trouble getting it, anxiety in keeping it, temptations in the use of it, guilt in the abuse of it, sorrow in losing it, and perplexity in disposing of it."* One can be surrounded by all kinds of material things, and still sense that something is gnawing a hole in the heart.

Many Bible passages deal with the use of money and with our attitudes toward money. In the last part of this chapter we will look at a portion of 1 Timothy 6 and notice some attitudes that are to be avoided.

a. The tendency not to be contented (verse 6)

We are told that *"godliness with contentment is great gain."* There is *a satisfaction* which ought to characterize the child of God. We must not be satisfied with what *we are* (for there is always room to improve our character), but we should constantly work at being satisfied with what *we have*. Contentment does not come from having all our wants supplied; it comes instead from *reducing our desires* to include only the essentials of life.

b. The notion that we can take it with us (verse 7)

We *"brought nothing into this world, and it is certain we can carry nothing out."* Every person comes into the world without a penny in his pocket; in fact, we come without a pocket in which to put a penny. And all of us will leave the world without taking any material goods with us. We can gather little or much between birth and death, but in the final hour, we will leave it all behind.

c. An excessive desire for unnecessary things (verse 8)

If we have "food and clothing" we are to be content. The word "clothing" is plural and means "coverings." It refers to both clothing and shelter. If we have food, clothing, and shelter—we should be satisfied. Our heavenly Father knows that we need all these things.

It is easy in this age of plenty to become obsessed with the desire to gorge ourselves with unnecessary things—many of which soon become more stuff to sell at the next garage sale. Material things can really get a tight grip on us. It is easy to think that we must have expensive furniture, sleek automobiles, restored antiques, extravagant holidays, up-to-date hunting equipment, etc.

The two factors that have a tremendous impact on the buying habits of multitudes of people in the western world are the *supermarket* and the *credit card*. Two cautions will help us to be wise in responding to these blessings.

1) Don't shop at the supermarket when you are hungry.

2) Don't use a credit card unless for convenience and then pay the balance in full each month.

d. Evils that attend a craving to be rich (verses 9-10)

Those who crave riches "fall into temptation and a snare, and into many foolish and harmful lusts which drown men in destruction…For the love of money is a root of all kinds of evil, for which some have strayed from the faith…and pierced themselves through with many sorrows."

What are some of the evils brought on by an undue love of money?

A long list could be given. *Greed for money* leads to selfishness, cheating, fraud, perjury, robbery, envy, quarreling, hatred, violence, and even murder. Greed lies behind *drug-pushing, pornography, the exploitation of the weak, the neglect of good causes, and the betrayal of friends.* Many television preachers have fallen for the idea that they must have private luxury jets to travel from place to place.[7]

The desire for riches is one of Satan's snares. Pursuing riches has brought many to spiritual destruction. Sometimes people have *deceived, defrauded,* and *cheated*—all to get more wealth. Verse 10 clearly states that it is not necessarily *an abundance* of money, but *the love of money,* which often leads to *lying, stealing, and prostitution.* And so indeed, the love of money is a root of all kinds of evil. Greed for money

---

[7] *World* Magazine, July 12/19, 2008 (pages 41-42) has a feature article describing the jets used by many televangelists.

has lured people into *gambling, fraud, arson, perjury, theft, and even murder.*

Multitudes who violate God's laws to get money and material things, have *"pierced themselves through with many sorrows"* (verse 10b). Those sorrows include the *tragedy* of a wasted life, the *sorrow* of losing children to the world, and the *grief* of seeing their wealth vanish over night. All of us must guard against becoming obsessed with material comforts, and with a desire to gorge ourselves with trivial things. A good philosophy is this: "Use it up; wear it out; make it do; do without."

The dedicated Christian must come to recognize that his wealth is for *sharing*, and not primarily for *hoarding*. Jesus said, "It is more blessed to give than to receive" (Acts 20:35).

Those who are rich in this world are *not to be "haughty, nor to trust in uncertain riches, but in the living God" (1 Timothy 6:17).* Not all of the early Christians were peasants and slaves; some were people of great wealth. *They were not rebuked for being wealthy, nor is it suggested that they should give away all their possessions.* They are simply instructed *not to trust* in them. One of the great snares of riches is that it's difficult to have them without trusting in them.

The term "uncertain riches" means that they are here today and gone tomorrow. The word "haughty" means "to be proud"—as if they deserved the riches. God often gives riches as a reward for thriftiness and hard work. The person who increased his five talents so that they became ten talents (Matthew 25:14-30), was rewarded for his diligence—and just so, the Lord often blesses those who are diligent and frugal. But the people who *love* money, even if they earn it honestly, can easily become a slave to it. It's easy to stray from the faith and backslide from God.

111

The clause, "who gives us richly all things to enjoy" (1 Timothy 6:17), means that *good and proper things in life are to be used and appreciated without feelings of guilt.* This includes *food*, *exercise*, *nature*, *vacations*, and *rest*.

The statement in verse 17 is not intended to condone luxurious living, but *it does provide balance* to those who might want to use verse 8 to insist that we must live in mud houses and walk barefooted in summer-time so that we don't have to buy as many shoes.

(6:18-19) Let them do good, that they be rich in good works, ready to give, willing to share, storing up for themselves a good foundation for the time to come, that they may lay hold on eternal life.

The wealthy are exhorted to "do good" and to be "rich in good works." They are to be generous with their giving, using money *to do good works*—such as supporting missionaries, spreading the gospel, and helping the needy. Those who give generously to support the cause of Christ will lay a foundation for the world to come. It will bring blessings in both worlds. "Eternal life" (verse 19b) is life everlasting—life that is *really* life—life that goes on forever!

Each of us needs to strive for a happy median regarding material things, seeking *to be thrifty without being miserly.* Proverbs 30:8-9 provides a good balance. If one is poor, there may be a temptation to steal; if one is rich, there may be a tendency to think he can get along without God, and perhaps deny any need for God. It is best for most of us just to have the simple necessities of life—no more and no less. So it is well to pray, "Lord, help us to escape the *dangers* of prosperity, and save us from the *desperations* of poverty."

Chapter 9

CARING FOR OLDER PARENTS

One of the problems that confronted the early church at Ephesus was that of caring for destitute widows. There were no pensions; there was no Social Security; there were no retirement homes. There were no honorable jobs for women.

Most churches today, regardless of size, have some older widows in their ranks—and widows say that *they are often forgotten after the first year following their husband's death.*

God has always expected His people to care for widows who are older. In the Old Testament, instructions were given in Exodus 22:22-24; in the New Testament the teachings for families and for the church are recorded in 1 Timothy 5:3-16 and in Mark 7:9-13.

God's people are told to honor widows who are up in years, and are not only bereft of their husbands, but are bereft of everything. They are "really widows" (1 Timothy 5:3-5). Such widows are desolate. They are widows who have no children and no money, and thus need special help.

1) The church is to care for widows who are bereft of family members and of financial security.

The church has a definite responsibility toward older persons who have no children or grandchildren who can care for them. There are two very clear responsibilities:

The church is to show honor, especially to destitute widows (1 Timothy 5:3). The widow is not to be looked down upon because she is poor. The word "honor" means to revere and to venerate even to the point of giving proper recognition and financial support.

113

The church is to bring relief for aged widows when there are no children or grandchildren. The Greek word translated "grandchildren" ["nephews" in 1 Timothy 5:4, KJV] literally means "descendants"—and thus refers especially to children and grandchildren. Christians in the local assembly have the responsibility of giving financial aid (and physical care) to widowed persons when there are no offspring that should be caring for those needs.

2) Family members are to aid and care for their older parents when they become more feeble.

The church has a responsibility toward aged widows who are completely desolate, but if they have offspring who are able to care for them, then the church does not need to assume that responsibility.

Jesus plainly condemned the Pharisees because they used a device known as "Corban" to evade responsibility toward their parents.[8] The word "Corban" is the Aramaic word for "gift."

If a Pharisee had an aged parent, and he did not want to help support that parent, he pledged his money to the Temple, and said "It is Corban" ["It is a gift to the Temple"]. Then he would say to his parents, *"My money is a gift dedicated to the Lord, and so I cannot use it to help you."* Read the account in Mark 7:6-13. It sounded very pious to speak of a gift to the church, but real piety will never allow aged parents to suffer from lack of care.

---

[8]   There is a new phenomenon in America today called "granny dumping." Older Americans are being shockingly abandoned in growing numbers; most are deposited at hospital emergency room doors. The *Newsweek* magazine has declared that there are growing numbers of children who "regard aging parents as a nuisance" (*Newsweek*, December 23, 1991).

114

The word "repay" (1 Timothy 5:4) means "to pay back for a benefit." It was our mothers and fathers who clothed and sheltered and nurtured us when we were young; they saw that food was on the table at mealtime; now we can do no less than help shelter and care for our mothers and fathers in their older age. In fact, *to act reverently* toward aged parents is *showing piety* in our homes. God will bless children who show proper love and mercy at home.

3) Today there are pensions, and there are rest homes [nursing homes] that will care for the aging.

Most older persons prefer to stay in their own homes, places where they had lived for many years. If they become incapacitated, they sometimes will choose the in-home care provided by groups organized for providing such care.

Other older parents will prefer to live in one of the retirement communities which are widely available today. Still others will opt to stay with family members who might be willing to care for them in old age.

A true Christian *widow* will trust in God and will pray often, and *God will use the church* as a channel for bringing an answer to her prayers (1 Timothy 5:5-6). Timothy is to teach the responsibility of *children* to support their older parents, and of the *church* to care for widows who are bereft of everything (verse 16). Only needy widows who had no other means of support were helped by the church.

God pronounces a severe condemnation upon those who are not willing to provide for the needs of their own family members (1 Timothy 5:8). Even most heathen people often have enough family love to provide for their family members. To fail to provide for our aging dependents means that we are worse than infidels.

The heart of Jesus was especially with widows. We see His concern for widows in the raising of the son of the widow of Nain (Luke 7:11-15), and in His praise for the widow who gave "two mites" (Luke 21:1-4). We have just noted too that Jesus scolded the Pharisees and teachers of the law for using the exemption known as "Corban" to give to the religious establishment instead of caring for the needy family members (Mark 7:9-13).

First Timothy 5 teaches that a widow's lonely life can blossom into a thing of beauty, if her time is devoted to prayer (verse 5) and Christian service (verses 9-10). These are spiritual ministries that we should encourage older believers to practice.

The Psalmist wrote some beautiful words about faithful saints who grow old: *"The righteous shall flourish like a palm tree, [they] shall grow like a cedar in Lebanon. Those who are planted in the house of the LORD shall flourish in the courts of our God. They shall still bear fruit in old age; they shall be fresh and flourishing"* (Psalms 92:12-14).[9]

Whether an older parent lives by himself, or in a retirement home, or in the home of one of his/her children—the parent has certain basic needs. We are not honoring our father and/or mother unless we do what we can to see that those needs are met.

---

[9] The *Life Application Bible* (NRSV) has an appropriate note on Psalm 92:14. "Honoring God is not limited to young people who have unlimited strength and energy. Even in old age, devoted believers can produce spiritual fruit. There are many faithful older people who still have a fresh outlook and can teach us from a life-time experience of serving God. Seek out an elderly friend or relative to tell you about their experiences with the Lord [and let them] challenge you to new heights of spiritual growth."

CONCLUSION

There are eight Beatitudes for friends of the aged to keep in mind as they attempt to minister to older persons as part of their service for Christ and the church.

1. Blessed are they who understand my faltering step and palsied hand.

2. Blessed are they who know that my ears today must strain to catch the things that others say.

3. Blessed are they who seem to know that my eyes are dim and my wits are slow.

4. Blessed are they with a cheery smile, who stop to chat for a little while.

5. Blessed are they who never say, "You've told that story twice today."

6. Blessed are they who know the ways to bring back memories of yesterdays.

7. Blessed are they who make it known that I'm loved, respected, and not alone.

8. Blessed are they who ease the days on my journey Home in loving ways.

--adapted and edited, author unknown

There are some ways that adult children can help their aging parents.

1. Communicate often.
Keep in touch by telephone, visits, and letters. Remember holidays, birthdays, and anniversaries.

2. Respect independence.
As long as possible, your parents need to make their own decisions about where and how to live.

3. Support "letting go."
Help them find constructive ways to dispose of their possessions by alerting them to thrift stores or mission programs that can benefit from the contributions.

4. Encourage reminiscing.
Draw forth from them memories of the past, and help them to fit together the pieces of their experiences.

5. Listen to them.
Hear the accounts of their past disappointments, accomplishments, and satisfactions, even if told repeatedly.

6. Encourage spiritual growth.
Help them to find sermon tapes, large print Bibles, enriching radio programs, and Christian newsletters. Provide transportation to attend church services.

7. Support usefulness.
Seek their counsel, praise their hobbies, and encourage their giving service to others.

---adapted from *Decision* magazine, May, 1998

BIBLIOGRAPHY
Marriage, Family, and the Christian Home

Bowman, Carl F. *Brethren Society:The Cultural Transformation of a Peculiar People*. Baltimore: Johns Hopkins Press, 1995.

Christenson, Larry & Nordis. *The Christian Couple*. Minneapolis, MN: Bethany Fellowship, 1977.

Christenson, Larry. *The Christian Family*. Minneapolis, MN: Bethany Fellowship, 1970.

Coblentz, John. *Christian Family Living (Second Edition)*. Harrisonburg, VA: Christian Light Publications, 2002.

Cornes, Andrew. *Divorce & Remarriage: Biblical Principles and Pastoral Practice.* Grand Rapids: Wm. B. Eerdmans, 1993.

Dobson, James C. *Love for a Lifetime: Building a Marriage that will go the Distance*. Portland, OR: Multnomah Press, 1987.

Dresher, John M. *For the Love of Marriage*. Intercourse, PA: Good Books, 1996.

Dresher, John M. *Parents—Passing the Torch of Faith*. Scottdale, PA: Herald Press, 1997.

Eden, Dawn. *The Thrill of the Chaste*. Nashville: W. Publishing Group [Thomas Nelson], 2006.

Elliot, Elisabeth. *The Shaping of a Christian Family*. Nashville, TN: Thomas Nelson Publishers, 1992.

Evans, Anthony T. *Guiding Your Family in a Misguided World*. Colorado Springs, CO: Focus on the Family, 1991.

Getz, Gene A. *The Christian Home in a Changing World*. Chicago: Moody Press. 1972.

Handford, Elizabeth Rice. *Me? Obey Him? The Obedient Wife and God's Way of Happiness in the Home*. Murfreesboro, TN: Sword of the Lord Publishers, 1972.

Hendricks, Howard & Jeanne, General Editors. *Husbands and Wives: A Guide to Solving Problems and Building Relationships*. Wheaton, IL: Victor Books, 1988.

Hostetter, Charles B. *How to Build a Happy Home*. Grand Rapids, MI: Zondervan Publishing House, 1960.

Huggett, Joyce. *Life in a Sex-Mad Society*. Glasgow, Scotland: Harper Collins Manufacturing, 1988.

Kauffman, Daniel. *Timely Talks with Teenagers*. Sugarcreek, OH: Schlabach Printers, n.d.

Kniss, Lloy A. *Practical Pointers for Training Your Child*. Harrisonburg, VA: Christian Light Publications, 1975.

Lessin, Roy. *Spanking: Why? When? How?* Minneapolis, MN: Bethany Fellowship, 1979.

LaHaye, Tim and Beverly. *The Act of Marriage: The Beauty of Sexual Love*. Grand Rapids: Zondervan Publishing House, 1976.

Lockyer, Herbert. *All the Promises of the Bible*. Grand Rapids: Zondervan Publishing House, 1962.

McDonald, Cleveland. *Creating a Successful Christian Marriage*. Grand Rapids: Baker Book House, 1975.

Miles, Herbert J. *Sexual Happiness in Marriage, Revised Edition*. Grand Rapids, Zondervan Publishing House, 1979.

Moore, J. H. *Our Saturday Night*. Elgin, IL: Brethren Publishing House, 1910.

Otto, Donna. *The Stay at Home Mom*. Eugene, OR: Harvest House Publishers, 1991.

Reapsome, James & Martha. *Marriage: God's Design for Intimacy*. Downers Grove, IL: InterVarsity Press, 1986

Rice, John R. *God in Your Family*. Murfreesboro, TN: Sword of the Lord Publishers, 1971.

Rosemond, John. *Parenting by the Book*. New York: Simon and Schuster, 2007.

Showalter, Lester. *What About Boy-Girl Friendships?* Crockett, KY: Rod & Staff Publishers, 1982.

Stormer, John A. *Growing Up God's Way: A Guide to Getting Children Ready for Life*. Florissant, MO: Liberty Bell Press, 1984.

Sweeting, George. *Special Sermons on the Family*. Chicago, IL: Moody Press, 1981,

Taylor, Robert R., Jr. *Christ in the Home*. Grand Rapids: Baker Book House, 1973.

Wenger, Ray M. *Divine Design for the Family*. Winona Lake, IN: Brethren Missionary Herald Books, 1990.

Wright, H. Norman. *Seasons of a Marriage*. Ventura, CA: Regal Books, 1982.

Wright, H. Norman. *The Pillars of Marriage*. Glendale, CA: Regal Books, 1979